MW00810668

A few words shared about the author...

Tom Llamas; American journalist for *ABC World News Tonight*:
   That is a **good** husband!

Cedric, the Entertainer; actor, stand-up comedian, and game show host:
   Every gesture of love he showed was **monumental**.

Angie Gaffney; Professional Certified Coach, film producer, executive director, and life/ leadership coach:
   Bob supported me in building a relationship with my husband, full of love, understanding, compassion, responsibility, and intimacy. **It is because of the work I did with Bob that my marriage evolved**—and my own evolution and desire for growth—gave my partner permission to do the same. My husband and I are now pursuing having children, I'm making more money than I ever have before, my well-being is stronger than it's ever been, and **there's so much more space in my life** for what I want to create moving forward.

Anthony Mason; American broadcast journalist for *CBS This Morning*:
   They're both (Bob Conlin and Shona Moeller) relationship coaches, and you can see why.

Scott Kallick; angel investor, adviser, mentor, and life/business/leadership coach:
   Bob helped me look at life in a more holistic way, which brought greater authenticity for me, and, ultimately, got me making decisions that served my happiness. **Bob is a skilled and purpose-driven coach.** Bob is a trusted adviser to me. **I heartily recommend Bob** to anyone looking to make positive changes in their life.

Dr. Lauren Borden; coach, public speaker, trainer, and consultant:
   Bob is so much heart, intuition, wisdom, and power. The insight he brings to our coaching sessions has been invaluable in helping me strengthen my relationships, build my business, and achieve my personal and professional goals.

Hayden Humphrey; uplifter, ex-corporate leader, and a recovering people pleaser:

> Working with Bob is like getting bear-hugged and walking across a finish line all at the same time. His insights, thoughtful questions, and powerful reflections enable you to access parts of yourself you didn't even know existed. His **presence lets you face the scary and overwhelming things while feeling safe and secure.**

Jenn Shull; professional ontological coach and certified yoga teacher:

> Bob Conlin of Conlin Coaching is **the real deal**—and by that, I mean he walks his talk.

Kristoffer "KC" Carter; author, meditation coach, and executive coach for Amazon and Edward Jones:

> Bob Conlin is a powerhouse coach and leader, full stop. Bob helped me look deep within my motivations (where I stop) and holds me to my highest and best. The breakthroughs we've achieved together will stay with me forever, as they affect my role as a dad, husband, shepherd, and teacher for my meditation students, coaching clients, and all my work impacts. I can't recommend Bob enough as a coach. He's a badass.

Joelle Goldstein; *People* magazine journalist and GLAAD Media Awards recipient:

> Conlin delivered.

WHY MY RELATIONSHIPS SUCK

CREATE STRONG RELATIONSHIPS WITH COURAGE AND HEART

Bob Conlin

Bob Conlin

Why My Relationships Suck Copyright @ Conlin Life Coaching, LLC
Conlin Life Coaching, LLC, Chicago, IL. All Rights Reserved

All rights reserved. No part of this book may be reproduced in any
form or by any electronic or mechanical means, including information
storage and retrieval systems, without permission in writing from the
author or publisher, except by reviewers, who may quote brief passages
in a review.

Paperback ISBN: 978-1-7370062-0-6

Editing and proofreading: T. Noble, Denise Michaels, Christine Manninen
Book cover design: WEIN Design Agency
Photo: KLEM Studios, LLC
Cover Photo By Prostock-studio; https://elements.envato.com

http://www.conlincoaching.com
http://www.wemeetagaincoaching.com
@relationship_alchemist (Instagram) #conlincoaching #livinginlove
Media and speaking:
Please contact bob@conlincoaching.com All other inquiries:
www.conlincoaching.com

Dedication

This book is about relationships. I've excelled at some and failed miserably at others. My goal in authoring this book is to share my experience, strength, and hope to create something new in how we give and receive love. What I've found in my journey and the journey of my courageous clients is that whatever you want is possible. So jump into the brave actions of doing. We have a relationship with everything and everyone. Our relationship with ourselves, those we love, and those we impact dramatically affect our life experiences. These relationships fundamentally impact the emotional, physical, and spiritual spectrum of what it means to be human. For better or worse, our relationships make life worth living. I could not have written this book without the help, love, and encouragement of so many. I also could not have written this book without being terrible in most of my relationships during my journey. My relationships with those I love, my careers over the years, and most importantly, my relationship with myself are the foundations upon which this project sits.

To the women who I loved and who loved me, thank you. Each experience in learning to love while with you is a gift. Every celebration, tear, heartbreak, fit of anger, and surrender toward forgiveness taught me what I wanted and what I didn't want; forever learning along the way—a little bit more of who I am, what I want, and how I want to give and receive love. As I fumbled along in our relationships, learning to love myself, I know I hurt many of you. I believe there's a gift within every heartbreak if we're courageous enough to receive it. The women I loved gave me many, but I thank you for ending our relationship when I didn't have the courage, providing a catalyst for my personal growth.

For my first relationship with another human being, I must thank my mom, Patricia. Our relationship as mother and son has encompassed every human emotion. Sometimes a comedy; sometimes a drama; sometimes a tragedy. We lived and learned through it all. You taught me tough love, a strong work ethic, to keep going no matter what, and to be a survivor. You helped me see that my self-destructive streak was leading me to a dead-end life. We've been the worst of enemies and the best of friends. Thank you for unconditionally loving me since the day I was born. I wouldn't be here if it weren't for you, and I mean that in every sense of those words. Thanks for never giving up on me and always seeing the good in me. Whenever I needed you, you were there. It is one of my greatest joys to have made and watch you be a grandmother.

Thank you to my older brother, Patrick. You taught me courage and how to stick up for myself, to finally say when enough is enough. Although I learned that lesson by throwing you against a refrigerator when I was thirteen, you nevertheless taught me that lesson. I love how our relationship has evolved over the years, and I'm so grateful to be as close as we are today. I cherish you, big brother, and I can never repay you for the kindness and generosity you've shown me, especially during the darkest hours of my life. You were there. You've always been my big brother, regardless of where our journeys have taken us. I can't wait to see what's next. It is one of my greatest joys to have made and watch you be an uncle.

To Dad, thank you. I wish we had more time together. You died when I was seven years old, and I've spent my whole life wondering what our relationship would have been like. Regardless, thank you for guiding and protecting me. Many circumstances in my life should have left me for dead, yet here I am. I owe that protection and safety to you. Thank you for being my guardian angel and whispering in my ear on the fourth date with Shona, "You're going to marry her." I needed that push. I was too scared to open my heart again, only to get hurt. I know your guiding hand has been at play my entire life. What I wouldn't give to have an hour with you, man to man, sharing it all. I love you.

To my stepfather, Jim, thank you for loving my mom, my brother, and me. I know I get my humor and wit from you. You've always been there for the three of us, and I'm so grateful you came into our lives. I was eleven years old when I met you, four years after my dad passed away. What I love most is that you never tried to take his place—not once. Thank you for making our family whole again. It is one of my greatest joys to have made and watch you be a grandfather.

To my healers and recovery communities, thank you. Special thanks to Kathy Metcalf for helping me start to heal and love my inner child. I could never explain in words how you've helped me. I genuinely believe God sent you as an angel. To Mara Stein, thank you for holding my wife and me during the most difficult time of our lives and relationship. You gave us hope and a place to process the many things we feared during our traumatic pandemic pregnancy. To those responsible for my intervention at work on January 25, 2007, you saved my life. To my sponsors and sponsees of my 12-step communities, I hear miracles through you and watch you live them. You've given me the courage to change the things I can.

Thank you to my very first coach, Dave Kehnast. Dave, you showed me what's possible when I get out of my way and that it's okay to be uncomfortable. You gave me the courage to make a few decisions that fundamentally altered my experience and life trajectory. I'm so glad I finally met you for coffee that Saturday morning. You're doing God's work. I often want to punch you in the face as you stand for my greatness. But you're easily in the top five when I think of the many people who've made an enormous difference in my life.

To my other coaches, Jenn Shull, Mark Hunter, and Hans Phillips, I could write an entire book on how each of you supported me and helped me create the future of my dreams; it was a future I thought was impossible, yet here I am creating it every day. Each of you made a profound impact.

Jenn, thank you for connecting me to Spirit and the wholeness of all of me. You showed me having emotions is part of being human, and as long as I can create the vision, I can achieve the experience.

Mark, thank you for supporting me in the rigor of self-love, and leadership and empowering the "15 Minutes of F*ckery." The breakthroughs I experienced while working with you made me a better leader, man, husband, and adult to my inner child.

Hans, thank you for supporting my foundation of well-being and integrity. Thank you for making success simple and look so dang easy and fun. Finally, thanks for helping me to become the father I'm today to a miracle baby. I love you all.

Thank you to my Accomplishment Coaching family. They gave me the skills to serve from my heart and authenticity. I wish everyone could experience the ontological training in the boot camp of love and being in our work. Thank you for being a flashlight for me to see both the greatness and blind spots of my humanity. Thank you for introducing me to my essence, my survival mechanism, and my purpose for being on this planet. This training was hands down, the best investment in my life. Thanks to Jodi Larson for making such a difference in all areas of my life: for being a friend, colleague, and champion. You're truly a Jedi angel. You've made such an impact in a simple, single statement many times by saying what needed to be said. Thanks to Rodney Mueller for supporting my inner child work and demonstrating the influence a kind man can have as an impactful leader. Thanks to Christina Stathopoulos for being my ontological, weirdo, ride-or-die sister and for not stopping with me in all the ways—always; to Laura Westman for getting me and letting me get you. To Lisa Pachence, thank you for saying to me what no one else would.

Thank you to my Leader-in-Training Colleagues and Mentor Coach colleagues for being on the wildest ride of our lives, experiencing breakdown after breakdown and breakthrough after breakthrough. Thank you to Christopher McAuliffe for having a dream and vision to create this fantastic company. They have made such a difference for so many. I hope you truly see the positive impact you make. I love you all.

Thank you to Lisa Almquist, Bee Bowman, Melanie Paez, and Emily Juricek for being beacons of love, light, and possibility during the scariest time of my life. You were Forest's earthly guardian angels. While we fought for our baby's life in those early days, your loving comfort kept us going. Thanks for teaching us how cosmic babies are, the power of music to heal, and for sharing stories about Forest that came to you in dreams. You'll never know the comfort you gave Shona and me.

Thanks to Denise Michaels, my book coach, for not giving up on me or this project. Your support and belief kept me going over these two years. Your insight and guidance into the message this book provides are as much yours as they are mine. Thank you, eternally. You have a gift for helping others get their book out of them. You'll be a lifelong colleague in my writing endeavors. I'm grateful our paths crossed.

Shona, my dear sweet, brilliant, courageous, gorgeous, hilarious, kind, and patient wife, thank you for loving me and taking exquisite care of my heart. Thank you for holding the space for all of me—the light and loving and the cruel and dark. Thanks for your constant call forth and for helping me see that I must be lovable if a woman like you chooses to love a man like me.

Watching you love me helps me learn to love myself daily. Every relationship of my life led me to you and our relationship adventures. I spent my whole life becoming the man capable of loving you and will spend the rest of it doing so. Manifesting our relationship has been my best creation. I love you.

To my in-laws, thank you for letting this big, tattooed, moody, smart-ass weirdo into your family. I've so enjoyed getting to be part of the family. You've helped me tap into parts of me that were always there but rarely expressed. Thanks for gifting me with my first chainsaw and having land that provides plenty of opportunities to use it. I so enjoy helping and contributing. I look forward to growing with all of you.

Thank you to my clients and all those with whom I've had the pleasure of having a conversation (whether we worked together or not). I could not be living my purpose without your courage to begin your developmental work. Creating a strong relationship with oneself, I believe, is one of the most courageous acts a person can take on. I 'm proud of you. I'm amazed by you. I'm grateful to you.

Finally, to my sweet boy, Forest—when I started drafting this book, you were far from being born. Mom and I didn't even know that we wanted you. We hadn't chosen you yet. Yet, you've taught me so much in the short time you've been here. The greatest gift you taught me was that I was already your father the moment I was born. Much like spending my whole life in relationships to learn how to love your mom, I was also learning how to be your dad. Although I was your father since the day I was born, I was just too scared to believe it. Thank you for your patience and for making me a father in the most miraculous way during the most miraculous time. You're the best creation I've ever created. Thank you for reminding me that miracles are real, magic is everywhere, and anything is possible. You're truly a miracle. I love you.

To Love
To Shona
To Forest
To Courage
To You

Foreword

As I sat on the couch, nursing a cold, I thought, "Why the hell not?" and opened my Tinder app. As usual, I expected to see the same old pictures of guys—topless, standing in front of a mirror, or taking a selfie in the driver's seat—always paying little attention to the description of themselves or the partner they ultimately wanted to spend the night with. This was, after all, a dating app for hookups.

I heard through the grapevine that there were unicorns on the site looking for a relationship. Until that fateful night in October, I hadn't seen that unicorn. In fact, I hadn't met any unicorns for more than one hundred fifty first dates. I was emotionally drained from years of dating—a cycle that looked more like a roller coaster than love life. But this year was different; I was different.

I was more empowered in my love for myself than ever. That's why I was not surprised when I saw a bright-smiling man with an incredible description of himself and what he wanted glow on my screen. His smile whispered, "I'm the man you're going to marry." I was intrigued. After all, he was nothing—and I mean **nothing**—like the men I dated before (except the bald head). He was full of tattoos (a broad-shouldered beefcake full of tattoos), but his profile shared deep insights into who he was and what he wanted his partner to be. It was an immediate yes!

Earlier that year, I declared I would hire a matchmaker or life coach to support my personal development and love life. Wouldn't you know—this smiley unicorn was a life coach. I couldn't believe it, so I swiped right without even thinking if we would match. Surprisingly, we did, and I received an immediate message from this tattooed, rocker beefcake about how he'd just returned from a week-long hiking trip on Isle Royale. He was speaking my love language. When I saw his smile via his profile picture, I felt my relationships wouldn't suck anymore. My feeling was confirmed, and I'm beyond grateful my relationships haven't sucked ever since.

Bob and I both genuinely believe we had to put in the work to love ourselves wholly before we could meet. Before individually diving into our inner work, we wouldn't have been equipped to fully express the love we now share. Bob loves hard, soft, sexy, and with totally unique magic. He is hyper-masculine (often mistaken for a biker dude) while embracing his feminine, Universal energies. Simply put, he is a unicorn; Bob is a rare species of a man who embodies the empowered balance of masculine and feminine energy—a grounded, goal-oriented doer who is a present, highly intuitive, heavy-metal-slinging, badass—and he's mine.

As you'll witness along your journey in *Why My Relationships Suck*, Bob's superpower is his understanding of how individuals love each other. His clients feel cared for, understood, respected, validated, and reassured. It's his gift. He'll take you on rides you never imagined while relating them back to you, using **his** past as a narrative to help you heal **yours** so you can create a future worthy of you.

Suppose you're stuck and unfulfilled in relationship after relationship that sucked. If this is your story, Why My Relationships Suck will shed light on where to focus your inner work and how to create the relationships you desperately crave. These relationships take courage, fearlessness, and massive doses of heart. Whether you find yourself (a) in-between relationships after declaring you'll never date again, (b) in a relationship as you begin your love journey, or (c) exiting a relationship that doesn't work anymore, this book will create a connection between your head and heart to ultimately expand who you are for yourself and others. You'll love deeper. You'll heal. Your heart will expand to create magic everywhere.

This book (filled with brutally honest, transformational, and soul-spilling stories from Bob's life) combines tales of sucky, relatable past relationships with the wisdom he learned throughout his life and leadership training. You'll laugh and find yourself in tears. Bob will speak to your heart—even if you've built miles-thick, protective walls. Your experiences will be normalized as you take a journey that pushes you past what you know, allowing you to expand your capacity to fully accept yourself and create powerful relationships. One of these relationships is the most important: it's the relationship you have with yourself.

Love and courage,
Shona Moeller

CONTENTS

Introduction

> Our relationship with ourselves impacts every other relationship we have. From within ourselves, all love begins. The greatest gift we can give to those we say we love and decide to love is to move into choosing a conversation appreciating the ways we love ourselves. Everything you need to create the love you want; you already possess.
>
> - Bob Conlin

This is a book about relationships—a book I never knew I had within and clumsily stumbled into writing. Honestly, I resisted this book the entire time I wrote it. In my lifelong quest to be loved, I learned so much about what to do and what not to do. I made so many mistakes. Ultimately, I had to learn to forgive myself and accept the compassion I usually didn't offer others, especially those who broke my heart. Ultimately, I had to learn how to love myself in my relationship journey.

I learned a lot about myself in my self-development journey, which began in the fall of 2015. I was at another crossroad: unfulfilled in my romantic relationship, miserable in what I thought was a dream job, and tortured by an incessant, negative voice in my head that questioned every thought, decision, or action. I also learned that many of my relationships shared a pattern; they all ended. Sometimes they ended dramatically; other times, they just died slowly. Months or even years of discontent, confusion, and unmet needs fueled heartbreak after devastating heartbreak. I didn't understand why I couldn't find what I wanted when it came to love. There was a constant longing and knowing that there was something more. Why couldn't I feel whole, complete, and happy in a relationship? Was I truly as unlovable and broken as my negative mindset and inner critic would have me believe?

For most of my life, many of these questions went unanswered. Then one day, a realization hit. The common denominator in all those sucky relationships—was me. It hit like a ton of bricks. If all my relationships started and ended the same way, it made sense to go deep within myself to discover what the hell was recreating my heartbreak, a cycle of having one failed relationship after another failed relationship. Part of me knew these relationship problems were of my making. Another terrified part didn't want to begin that journey because I wanted to put all responsibility on my past partners.

I knew I needed to change. I had to do something different if I wanted something different. More importantly, it was time to **be** someone different. Who I was in relationships wasn't working. How I showed up, my energy, my commitment, and the way I created partnerships was bankrupt. I felt like I was finally given a consequential invitation to look inward. So I began swallowing huge chunks of truth about myself. I dove headfirst into ontological coaching, cognitive behavioral therapy, and 12-step work. (Ontological coaching refers to coaching to ways of being, the energy we bring forth, as a means to produce major shifts in perception and behavior.) This uncomfortable journey became my invitation to take responsibility for the beginning of my healing, coaching, and spiritual journey. That journey led and continues to lead to the most fulfilling, loving, and nurturing relationship I've ever had. At forty-two years old, I'm finally figuring this love thing out.

You need to discover what's in the way of the love you want. The discovery is about creating an awareness of **the gap** (as we call it in coaching), then acting in service to achieve your relationship goals. The gap is an invitation to new, uncomfortable actions to develop new, likely, however uncomfortable, results. Sometimes getting exactly what you want can be uncomfortable. It can also be what stops you before even starting.

What if I meet the person I want to spend the rest of my life with? Will I be ready? This book is about bringing intention, clarity, and direction into the magic that is love. With this support, you can begin taking responsibility for creating your future. A future you have absolute control over and one where all possibilities exist. The way to predict your future is to create it.

First, you need to create a loving relationship with yourself. All relationships are impacted by the relationship you have with yourself. It's a vitally important truth. Whenever I'm struggling in any relationship (romantic, collegial, familial, or platonic), I've learned to point the finger at myself first. The old cliché "How can you love someone else if you don't love yourself?" is true. There are some conditions to this wisdom: you must learn to love yourself. Each of us has the opportunity to love, accept, and forgive ourselves. To get into a compassionate relationship with yourself is to love yourself freely into the reciprocal love of our partners, families, and friends.

I share my journey through my first love, tragic divorce, recovery, and experience of doing the necessary work to meet my current wife. I share the courageous stories of coaching clients and thousands of conversations with others in their quest for love. I've changed the names of previous partners to protect their privacy and adhere to the confidentiality agreements I have with clients. You'll see yourself in the stories shared on these pages. I hope you get some gold nuggets from their wisdom or empathize with the heartbreak of their folly. This book is a guide to creating strong relationships with courage and heart. You'll discover how to:

◆ Be **the one** for you first.
◆ Let go of the past.
◆ Change your beliefs about heartbreak.
◆ Transform into a person who desires, demands, and believes the love you deserve is possible; and
◆ Find love and commitment that works for you.

I am one man with many stories and with many clients. My clients and I have had success learning how to create the love we want with others while learning to love ourselves along the way. I invite you to keep an open heart and mind. Take from this book what works for you and leave the rest. Refer to this book when you're challenged in a relationship, and consider it a lifelong reference—a textbook, if you will. Highlight the parts that speak to you. Bookmark them and keep them close as you navigate your next or current relationship in this new way.

I aim to make the lessons in this book resonate with you and challenge you. While this book is written largely from my heteronormative experience, my wish is that anyone committed to creating a powerful and fulfilling relationship derives value from it. I hope this book calls you forth to step further outside your comfort zone than you ever have before. I also hope you swallow some chunks of truth about yourself and take 100 percent responsibility for the love you yearn to create. This book is about (*a*) possibility, (*b*) daring to dream, and (*c*) welcoming the experience and wisdom to support you in creating a solid relationship with courage and heart. Enjoy the process, and the best of luck as you begin your journey toward love and happiness.

CHAPTER ONE

THE END WHERE IT ALL BEGAN

> "Start where you are. Use what you have. Do what you can."
> - Arthur Ashe

Pressing repeat on the saddest song in my playlist, I cried. I was back in the familiar place of another failed relationship. This one ended in a slow, dying manner that, in the end, fizzled out and disappeared. Calls stopped, texts stopped, and when I saw her in public, it was like I was a stranger. Now in my forties, the possibility of ever having a relationship worthy of me (one I genuinely wanted) was becoming a fading possibility. There must be something wrong; there had to be.

My heart was broken again.

The devastation was different; as I cried for myself. It was the first time ever, after a breakup, the tears were for me. I was heartbroken for myself. Usually, the sadness was directed toward the person leaving and breaking my heart; however, that person was me this time. I was tired of being unable to love and be loved in a way that made a real difference. The women I was attracting, the man I was to attract, how I failed them, and failed myself was bankrupt. Something had to change to have a chance at ever finding meaningful love.

I thought Rachel was **the one**. She was the first woman I seriously dated after ending a long, seven-year relationship. Rachel met and exceeded many conditions I considered and wrote down on the list for an ideal partner. It was amazing being with a successful, brilliant, and hilarious woman. In the beginning, she tried to show her appreciation, which was a wonderful feeling. It felt nice to be appreciated again; however, our romance was swift, lasting only a few months. I immediately saw the warning signs of an impending heartbreak but ignored them.

I kept putting in the work, knowing it would inevitably end. What was more confusing was that when I became honest with myself, it was obvious she wasn't even close to what I truly wanted. She wasn't **the one**. So what made me stay? It was painful being with her but more painful being alone. The thought of being alone again was terrifying. I hit bottom and knew something had to change. I was done.

The breakup was the greatest gift I ever received in my desire to create love and a relationship. Hitting rock bottom from this heartbreak forced me to look at myself in a completely new way. I had to become honest and responsible. It never occurred to take some level of responsibility for my heartbreak. Playing the victim was easier than looking inward and being honest by acknowledging most of the relationship breakdown was because of me.

I received an invitation to work on myself. To ever truly create the relationship I wanted, I needed to explore myself in relationships, so the invitation was accepted. I took on the personal growth work and met and married the woman of my dreams close to a year later. I found love.

The Relationship Merry-Go-Round

I come from a long line of failed relationships. Before Rachel, it was a seven-year relationship with Amanda. Before Amanda, it was an eight-year relationship and marriage with Mary that ended in a divorce. A handful of other young-love relationships all had the same ending: failure. They failed in the sense that the relationships didn't last. In hindsight, these relationships provided invaluable teaching moments. Most of them ended with my partner leaving. While as a couple, we were amicable, the relationship ended with me feeling confused, distraught, heartbroken, and alone. I felt blame, shame, and guilt for causing the separations and for each person to fall out of love. I blamed myself when each one left.

We aren't doing a clinical study on what made all these relationships unexpectedly end. This journey through all those relationships led me to a place of love, understanding, and gratitude. Ultimately, I found myself through the process outlined in this book, and I'm sharing the process with you. Surprisingly, I also found and fell in love with myself. It guided me to the woman and relationship of my dreams. My way of doing relationships had to change. I had to change too, but how?

Asking for Help Sucks

Something had to change. My typical approach was to discover how to make things go differently, utilizing the exact same tools that landed me where I was. When approaching new relationships, I was the same old person but expecting different results. Many people say that's a definition for insanity: doing the same thing over and over but expecting different results. I was using the same road map, hoping to reach another destination. I would arrive at a similar X-marks-the-spot relationship outcome—bewildered and confused with my heart ripped from my chest.

"How did I get here?" I asked myself over and over.

One of the hardest issues was asking for help. I assumed I could just do the same thing except do it better, faster, or harder to get a new result. That was wrong. The carnage of failed relationships was all the proof necessary to finally realize that I needed help. I knew help was essential for a future relationship to ever be successful, and I was clueless about how or where to start. I kept looking for what could be done. Was there some new action or place to go outside myself? Through a stroke of luck, it became clear that where I must go was inward. I already possessed all the answers to the questions about love. I needed a guide to help find them.

Help came first in the form of Dave. Dave is a rebellious, renegade, magical, free-spirited, brilliant, and loving man. He's a bit of a punk-rock, spiritual hippie. I love this man and am so grateful he came into my life. He's also the person who openly says what no one else will. Sometimes I hate him for that. In the beginning of my journey, I kept bumping into Dave at random times and locations as each day, week and month were leading up to a big breakup. It was almost comical as if the Universe was setting up candid camera shots for a big love prank.

For example, I'd be at a stoplight on my bike, and Dave would pull up next to me. I'd be at a coffee shop and feel a tap on my shoulder. I'd walk into the gym, and he would be walking out. "Just checking out the place," he said. When we crossed paths, we'd chat for a bit; then, he'd ask me deep, meaningful questions that made me face the truth of my relationships. They were like laser incisions to break up the scar tissue to slowly open my heart. Why wasn't I living in love?

My gut said there was something to gain from this man. In the biggest cosmic joke of all, Dave was a life coach—a life coach? I remember thinking how ridiculous that sounded. What the hell is a life coach? Who works with a life coach and why? Despite my judgments, I took a chance and met Dave for coffee. That hour-long meeting changed the course of my life and the way I love. Dave became my first-ever life coach because I was at a crossroads in life. I had zero faith life coaching would help me, but didn't know what else to do, so I trusted him. I already had everything anyone could imagine (the lovely house, a nice car, a relationship, and an excellent job), yet I came home each night asking, "Is this all there is to life? There has to be more."

I felt unfulfilled and drained in most areas of life. Although I was in a relationship, I felt alone. Fulfillment wasn't about what I had. Fulfillment was about who I was and wasn't in this life. The new awareness began to direct my thinking and actions. During the time I worked with Dave, I quickly understood why I felt unfulfilled. My current relationship was what coaches call a power leak. My power, the ability to impact my experience, and love had a hole. The lack of fulfillment and happiness wasn't because of my partner but my reaction to the relationship we created. I was leaking personal power and felt helpless, stuck, confused, and unfulfilled.

After months of exploring what I **really wanted** and getting clarity around what I had, it became clear there was a gap. Dave asked a bold question. "So, is it over?"

"Is what over?" I replied, pretending not to know what he was talking about.

"Is the relationship over?" he asked.

"Well, if it doesn't drastically change, then it has to be," I mumbled to Dave through the beginning of fresh sobs.

That was the moment I had to choose. It was time to decide if I was willing to make a difference in the experience of the relationship I wanted or if I'd keep doing the same thing better, faster, or harder while expecting a new result. Insanity, remember? I was being asked to do this now—end the relationship now. Not later when it felt easier—but **right now**. It was incredibly uncomfortable. I had to repeatedly step into that same discomfort for any relationship to change, and I hated it. That night, I asked her to have a serious conversation. It was the beginning of the end.

After hours of therapeutic and coaching support, we ended our seven-year relationship a couple of months later. It was the most loving and amicable breakup I had ever experienced. We each (*a*) had our voice, (*b*) our say and (*c*) got to be ourselves. That doesn't mean it was easy, but it was kind, which allowed each of us to be with whatever came up as it came up. It was the most responsible I'd ever been in my life about a relationship... and it was ending.

I Needed a Relationship—to Fix Me

That breakup helped me realize a fundamental, uncomfortable truth: I approached relationships out of need. Whether emotional, physical, or mental, I needed a partner to fill a hole—to fix what was missing. There was a gap only a woman who loved me could fill. Time and time again, I relied too heavily on another to meet my needs to feel whole and complete. I often placed unrealistic expectations on these women. And 100 percent of the time, the expectations were never communicated. Here I was, putting unrealistic, **unspoken expectations** on them. It was the ultimate trap because they never had a chance.

These relationships were doomed to fail from the start. I hadn't yet realized to have a successful, loving, fulfilling relationship with someone I had to have one with myself first. I wanted something from these partners that I could only give myself first; that something was love.

I continued operating in deficit mode in relationships with others and myself. Neither my partner nor I was ever enough. This deficit created a consistent, constant feeling of lack and wanting. There was a gaping, black hole in my heart, and I sucked them in, tearing them apart while expecting them to fill it for me.

Left Foot...Right Foot

My relationship journey started when I began the journey of self-development. This internal exploration had me face every part of me: the good, the bad, the ugly, and the downright screwed up and wounded. I inventoried the past relationships, the present, and who I wanted to be in relationships. I enrolled in a rigorous, year-long training program to become a coach. **During** that process, I became so much more. The coaching made such a difference in my life. It became clear it was my calling to do the same for others.

Dave helped to clear a path for my future. As I learned to become a coach, I was reintroduced to myself. I explored who I needed to be, what I needed to learn, and the right questions to ask to make an impact for others. While learning how to help others, I also looked at how to help myself.

This program and experience was by far, hands down, the best investment I've ever made in myself. It was a year of exploration and coming to understand myself. It also was an opportunity to become responsible in relationships while gaining support and structure to dream up the relationship I genuinely wanted—a container of possibility.

Where Are You?

Let's get clear on the current state of your relationship. You'll need to know your starting point. This is the beginning of your journey, from where you'll take your first step. Most people are living in one of three experiences of a romantic relationship at any moment:

- ◆ You don't have a romantic relationship, and you want one.
- ◆ You have a romantic relationship you want to leave but don't know how.
- ◆ You have a romantic relationship you want to improve.

Wherever you're at in the three options above, there's a common thread: you. This is true of all your past, current, and future relationships. You (*a*) have been, (*b*) are, or (*c*) will be part of them. Yes, it sounds simple, but people are so often focused on the other half of the relationship as the problem/issue/drama that they don't take responsibility for themselves. *Why My Relationships Suck* requires you to take full responsibility for yourself and every aspect of your relationships.

CHAPTER TWO
WELCOME TO YOUR HEARTBREAK

> "Your task is not to seek for love, but merely to seek and find all the barriers within yourself that you have built against it."
> - Rumi

If you love, then your heart will get broken—guaranteed. Love is the greatest gift of being human, and it comes with the greatest cost. If you allow love into your life, your heart will be broken, and love will end. It's a fact. If your relationship lasts until the final minute of the final day your partner is alive, then the until-death-do-us-part of your vows will lead to heartbreak.

So why are we surprised when it happens? In love, heartbreak is inevitable. If your heart (*a*) has been broken, (*b*) is currently breaking, (*c*) is closed and damaged, or you feel you can't go on, then welcome. Welcome to your heartbreak. I'm glad you're here, and I want to acknowledge you. You're reading this book to do something about your broken heart. That takes courage, resilience, and determination. Celebrate this. I hope this book supports you on your journey to find the ability to love again fearlessly.

As you experience your heartbreak, the natural tendency is not to be with it. You ignore it, operate on top of it, or distract yourself, so you don't have to feel what you're feeling. This tendency is normal, and it's why your relationships suck. Heartbreak is a threat. Either you avoid the hell out of it or attack it with anger, resentment, and fear. You stuff the discomfort down and ignore the inevitable consequence of choosing love. You're protecting yourself, but that so-called protection comes at a cost. You never fully (*a*) deal with, (*b*) heal, and (*c*) learn from the experience. This is how we usually deal with a broken heart. There is a tremendous benefit to stepping into the discomfort of your heartbreak; it's self-love. Stepping in allows you to begin learning about and understanding yourself in ways only an experience like this can provide. Self-love will become a familiar choice for you and a catalyst for creating fulfilling relationships. You'll learn to love yourself and become the one for you. This supports you by building strong relationships with courage and heart.

Get in a Relationship with Your Heartbreak

I have an invitation for you. You may not like it, but I invite you to allow and embrace all of your heartbreak. Step in 100 percent and allow your heartbreak to happen freely. Feel every bit of it—every corner of your torn-apart, weeping heart—the dark, shielded, angry, devastated, I-will-never-love-again brokenness of it all. Sob uncontrollably. Scream until your throat hurts. Cry whenever and wherever. Get so angry you see red. Swear off love forever. Get it out. Feel it. Feel the thoughts of how (*a*) it went, (*b*) you'll never get over it, and (*c*) you were stupid and blind to let this happen. Feel all the missed opportunities to do, say, or be a different version of yourself that would have prevented the heartbreak. Feel the hollowness and tension in your body. Get it all out. When you think you're done, take another look within and feel more of however your heartbreak physically manifests itself. Be with it—all of it.

I'm sorry this happened or is happening to you. It will get better. Although you may not believe it will, it does. Take a moment to remember a time, perhaps the first time, when your heart was broken. How did it go? How is it now? It took time, right? Most of us get better most of the time on our own. Your heartbreak didn't last forever. You may seek professional help, a therapist, coach, or perhaps a doctor to get medical treatment, but you do get over it. We heal or move through it and just suck it up as we power through. You will too, but it's going to suck. Allow your heartbreak to completely happen. Embrace the suck.

Have you heard the saying, "Time heals all wounds?" Well, it will; I also believe in the healing process scar tissue develops. Like all deep wounds, scar tissue is left behind. Time will heal your wounds, but you've experienced a trauma, a wound to the heart. While that wound heals, you've either developed or will develop scar tissue in your healing process. Most deep wounds leave behind a mark as a memory of their existence. So wouldn't it make sense that there's an emotional scar left behind on your heart? To illustrate this, let's look at it another way and consider the largest organ of your body: your skin.

Has your skin ever been scarred? I bet you have a few scars on your body somewhere. Some old harms or traumas healed, but they forever changed you. Your skin is healed, but now it's no different. There's a mark—a scar signifying the event. You have a story to tell about how you got that scar. Maybe it was a clumsy fall, a dog bite, an unplanned appendectomy while home for the holidays, a fight you got into with a sibling, or an accidental cut you got while loading the dishwasher. However it happened, you likely have a scar somewhere on your body. It changed you, right? It has forever altered the look and feel of your skin, and you probably don't think much about it anymore.

This is how you can relate to your heartbreak. There will be a day when you won't think about it much, but it has shaped you. The look and feel of your heart is different. You have a story about that relationship and how it changed you forever. The heartbreak eventually heals, but it leaves behind a lesson. Those lessons can positively or negatively impact your relationships, and it's up to you to choose how you'll move into your next relationship with this experience. Learn from it. Grow and transform. Get over it before you drag the same heartbreak into your next relationship.

My First Time

My first heartbreak happened the summer between my sophomore and junior year of high school. I met Kim in the eighth grade. It was one of those "Hey, she thinks you're cute!" conversations from one of her friends. We soon met up after school and awkwardly talked. Kim was a jock with beautiful, long, curly hair. She was very fit and earned good grades. She also had a kind heart. I was a rocker with hair halfway down my back who wore heavy-metal t-shirts and had the biggest chip an angsty teen could have on their shoulder.

We were not supposed to be together or mix, as dictated by the social norms of our school. Jocks and rockers didn't belong together. We were the forbidden fruit, which fueled our obsession and eventual love for each of us to be together. This was the beginning of my first long-term, committed relationship. Kim and I grew up in our relationship and fumbled through early adolescence, making all the mistakes dumb kids make. We were (*a*) caught fooling around, (*b*) ditching school, and (*c*) getting dropped off at the movies only to leave through the back door to make out in the alley. Looking back, it was no wonder our parents did everything they could to never leave us alone.

Kim was the first girlfriend I loved. My heart hurt when I wasn't with her. I envisioned a future with her, one in which we would continue to grow together as we got older. We would get married after high school and have little jock and rocker kids. She was going to be a professional athlete, and I was going to play heavy metal on stages across the world in front of millions. My first love and high-school sweetheart was my everything. Looking back now, we were just two confused kids doing things neither of us should've been doing. There was a whole life ahead for each of us, but it was a life that didn't include us remaining together.

Kim taught me devastation and heartbreak, which I now realize were gifts in disguise. At the time, it felt like she gave me a death sentence, and I'd be alone and miserable forever. That experience introduced me to depths of sadness I never imagined experiencing. I convinced myself how unlovable I was, punished myself, made myself wrong, and headed down a path of self-destruction. I learned how much responsibility I heaped on myself for how those relationships went. I must have done something to cause the relationship to end. There must have been something wrong with me. I was terrible. It was all bullshit. My brain and heart were trying to make sense of what was happening, and they struggled. There was nothing wrong with me. I fell in love and hadn't yet learned that love always ends with a broken heart. It's part of the deal.

What the Hell is Happening to Me?

Heartbreak hurts, and there is no getting around it. If it's masked, medicated, or ignored, it will eventually catch up to you and either come out sideways in your next relationship or block you from creating your next one. This is precisely why I invited you to feel it all. Get it all out. Your body is experiencing your heartbreak in real-time, and physiological changes are happening. It's normal to emotionally, mentally, and physically feel how you're feeling during or after a breakup. This is your body's healing.

You're grieving the loss of your partner and the future you imagined the two of you would create together. It is over, and that finality creates a physiological response. This response is powerful and, at times, can be overwhelming. Understanding what's happening in the brain and body can be helpful in explaining what you're experiencing. It's normal to feel as horrible as you currently feel, have felt in the past, or may feel in the future. Even if you're not in the depths of heartbreak currently, understanding this will guide you as you process an old heartbreak or move through a new one.

Barbara Fane, a psychotherapist, summed up the body and brain's physiological responses to heartbreak in a 2016 article, "Grief Symptoms: How Grief Affects the Brain." Review the brief notes below and see if you can relate. Perhaps this will help you understand your thoughts, feelings, and bodily sensations as you move through a broken heart. Consider these brain areas and how scientists believe grief symptoms affect them.

◆ **The parasympathetic nervous system:** This section of your autonomic nervous system is in the brain stem and lower part of your spinal cord. In this system, which handles rest, breathing, and digestion, you may find that your breath becomes short or shallow, your appetite disappears or increases dramatically, and sleep disturbance or insomnia becomes an issue.

I found it so hard to sleep during my breakups. I was wired. All I wanted to do was sleep and pass the time. Not being awake to experience the hurt was a gift, yet getting adequate and restful sleep was often brutal.

◆ **The prefrontal cortex/frontal lobe:** The functions of this area include (*a*) the ability to find meaning, (*b*) planning, (*c*) self-control, and (*d*) self-expression. Scientific brain scans show that loss, grief, and traumas can significantly impact your emotional and physical processes. Articulation and appropriate expression of feelings or desires may become difficult or exhausting.

Self-control was nearly impossible. I'd call my exes and beg them to take me back, show up at their new boyfriends' houses, and engage in irrational behavior. I'd eat a dumpster full of garbage foods and sabotage anything good. I was like a wild animal.

◆ **The limbic system:** This is the emotion-related brain region (particularly the hippocampus) in charge of personal recall, emotion and memory integration, attention, and your ability to take an interest in others. During grief, it creates a sensory-oriented, protective response to your loss. Perceiving loss and grief as a threat, the amygdala portions of this system instruct your body to resist grief. You may experience intense, instinctual, or physical responses to triggers that remind you of your losses.

I remember completely resisting myself from experiencing my emotions fully. I just couldn't accept them or be with them. Instead, the resistance caused my feelings to boil over inside, and I'd explode into fits of anger and rage. Seeing a picture, passing by a favorite restaurant, or hearing a song would all trigger my broken heart to scream.

In a 2006 study, Helen E. Fisher, an American anthropologist, the chief scientific adviser for Match.com, a human behavior researcher, and a self-help author, noted that the brain releases similar chemicals for romantic breakups and romantic love. Her study, "Romantic love: a mammalian brain system for mate choice," was published in the Journal of Neurophysiology. These chemicals include pheromones, dopamine, norepinephrine, epinephrine, and serotonin. As dopamine and norepinephrine levels increase, serotonin levels decrease, and these changes are associated with increased heart rate, trembling, flushing, pupil dilation, sleeplessness, and loss of appetite.

You are physiologically reacting to your experience, which is exactly how it should be. Embrace it. Normalize it. Your body is built to feel what you're feeling. Your feel-good brain chemicals are low, and you're a bit anxious. Declare it as perfect. I found great comfort in understanding why I experienced things in a certain way. What was the science and biology behind my broken heart? It helped me understand the deep hurt, acting irrationally and feeling as if I'd never feel normal again. Go ahead and explore the science of your heartbreak a bit further to normalize your experience.

In reaction to these physical changes, there are several actions you can take to support yourself through the process. Don't give up on what makes you happy. Endorphins, the feel-good chemicals we all have, are naturally produced in your body. Your endorphins are a tremendous ally in your heartbreak process. Get moving! Exercise. Walk. Eat your favorite foods. Eat chocolate. Eat spicy foods. Sniff some essential oils like lavender or vanilla. Watch a funny movie. Surround yourself with a group of people who love you. Do the research and experiment with what works best for you. Commit to daily endorphin-boosting activities and behaviors because supporting your physical health provides an opportunity to take a deeper look inside.

Broken Heart Garden

Your heartbreak offers a lot of awareness and an opportunity for growth. It's the soil to grow, learn, and develop into the person you want to be in a relationship. This is fertile ground, so don't waste it. Perhaps there is a new awareness to generate and explore. Take stock of who you are while in a relationship. What can you own? Where can you be and do better? Notice your patterns and how you set yourself up for this. Normalize your experience and if you want to work toward a different experience in the future, then do something different.

- ◆ Remember these tips and truths:
- ◆ To love is to concede to future heartbreak.
- ◆ Heartbreak is inevitable, it's a normal life experience.
- ◆ Your body has a physiological response to heartbreak.
- ◆ Allow your body time to process what's happening.
- ◆ Heartbreak is an invitation to learn and grow.
- ◆ You'll repeat patterns if you don't change them.
- ◆ If you want a different relationship, take a different action.

Break on Through (to the Other Side)

On the other side of your heartbreak is your new beginning. The new beginning is filled with all the wonder, joy, and adventure of learning to love and be loved again. Love is the most rewarding aspect of the human experience. It is glorious; it's rediscovering the first kiss, exploring a new body, discovering commonalities, and challenging beliefs within your new partner. Their history combines with your history to form a unique present and possibly a future. You learn about yourself as you learn about your new partner—it's fantastic and a hell of a lot of fun! Take a moment to remember the elation, excitement, and animalistic nature that awakens: the hunt, the play, and the adventure. It will come back. Breathe that in and hope you'll find love—whether it's for the first time or once again.

Take your time and honor your heartbreak process. A mistake many make is not to allow your heart to heal, then quickly get involved in what will be another disaster of a relationship. There is a beautiful opportunity in your grief to fully express, discover, and allow all your heartbreak. If you're up to it, then take yourself on. Become an explorer of yourself and who you are while in your heartbreak experience. Engage this process like an adventure—just as you would climbing a mountain. Seek, uncover, and discover the territory of your heartbreak. What's your heartbreak teaching you about yourself?

Here's my invitation. Explore patterns that show up in your relationships and ask yourself:
- ◆ What is predictable? and
- ◆ Do you engage in sabotaging behaviors?

Then explore old wounds that haven't healed and ask yourself:
- ◆ What would help them to heal? and
- ◆ Are these wounds gnawing into other relationships?

While writing this book, I'd just signed a six-month contract with a new client named Tracy. I met her a year earlier at a mutual friend's wedding. She was brilliant, powerful, hilarious, beautiful, a great dancer, and, surprisingly, alone at the wedding. It was clear after a few sessions that something from her past was impacting her present. Tracy had a history of dating **emotionally unavailable** men. If she made it past a few dates with them and committed to being in a relationship with them, it always ended the same: she was left unfulfilled, confused, and heartbroken.

Tracy discovered her patterns of sabotage and how she was also emotionally unavailable. She would shut down and disengage with men she was honestly interested in. She would also create relationships with men who were nowhere near the type she wanted to be with. This was all an act to predict her future. She made an unwinnable game that would reliably end in disappointment and heartbreak. This was safe for her.

Tracy learned very early on that love and relationships were threatening. She created a defense, like a shield, to prevent her from building meaningful, lasting romantic relationships. After the first man she became very interested in was injured and unexpectedly died, she learned that the people she cares for would abandon her. She learned that love is dangerous and something to avoid. Did Tracy think this was still impacting her? Of course not, but when we went deep, we could see how she was still protecting her broken heart.

Tracy was unaware how her past was impacting her present and future. I invited her to seek therapy to support her in processing these defense mechanisms and finally begin her healing. I've found that those who use both therapy and coaching have access to incredible results as they create and maintain effective relationships and partnerships. Tracy has since learned how to create powerful, committed relationships. She became responsible for her broken heart as part of the cure to develop the relationship experience she truly desired.

What the Hell is Self-Love?

Have you fallen short of being all you need to be for yourself? I know I have. Suppose you don't begin to investigate the unresolved, negative beliefs that surround the way you think, feel, react, and behave. In that case, how you shape those personal experiences will continue to carry into your **next relationship**. It will follow you if there's a gap in how you relate to and love yourself. This gap will saturate your future relationship and get all over your future partner. Have you expected your partners to complete you by giving you a piece of yourself that you're missing? Were they expected to fix or distract you from yourself just long enough to avoid repeating old patterns? Take this time during your heartbreak to learn to love yourself—all of yourself.

What does self-love look like to you? Many of my clients have a self-love practice. Without fail, there is confusion as to what it means. Many believe there is a specific way to love oneself. That belief causes confusion, which leads to another belief that they must be doing it wrong. This cycle of belief and confusion creates another opportunity to make ourselves wrong, inadequate, and broken. This is false—so stop.

You get to choose what self-love looks and feels like. It's entirely up to you. Your brain will fight you. If you accept it, your challenge is to lean in and ask your heart for guidance. Turn your head off for this challenge. Perhaps self-love looks like eating a pint of ice cream, twenty extra minutes on the treadmill, or inviting a friend over to hug and hold you. Self-love can be anything you choose. Choose it intentionally, so you'll know it's happening when it occurs. You'll know—this is me loving myself.

Engage in the following activities to help you recognize what it looks like to love yourself:

◆ Discover what self-love looks like to you.
◆ Say positive affirmations daily.
◆ Engage in behaviors that care for your body, mind, and spirit.
◆ Practice gratitude when fear and judgment arrive.
◆ Write a daily gratitude list.
◆ Be intentional with your self-love actions.
◆ Use the evidence of these actions to know you're loving yourself.

More About Me...

Kim and I got back together a few times after the breakup. We grew a bit older together, but it never worked out. I still wonder why she ended our relationship, but it doesn't matter. In hindsight, I'm grateful that she did because I learned more from this relationship than any other relationship since. Reflecting on this relationship was pivotal to learning about my broken parts and where my opportunities were to improve myself. Although it took years and several other failed relationships, I finally dared to begin my self-development journey.

Feel your heartbreak, then challenge yourself to love yourself through it every day. Allow all of it. I still feel mine daily. I take on this work with my wife—my partner—the woman of my dreams who knows and loves all of me because I know and love all of myself. I fully express myself, aware of who I am and who I'm not, as a person who was shaped throughout life, in and out of relationships. Choose to be 100 percent responsible for your relationship. If you're willing, then keep reading. If not, give yourself more time to grieve and come back when you're ready. This book will be waiting for you.

CHAPTER THREE
RESPONSIBILITY

> You're only a victim to the degree of what your perception allows.
> - Shannon Alder

Warning: there is a strong possibility this chapter will trigger you. The reason all your relationships suck is because of you. You suck, you've sucked, or you'll continue to suck until you take responsibility. We've confirmed a critical point if that statement causes a stirring inside. Not only do you suck, but you're also a victim.

I'm being blunt to prove a point. It's up to you to make your relationships occur differently, starting now. Right now, it's time to take responsibility for how all your relationships have or have not occurred up until this moment. Remember, the common thread in all your relationships is **you**. So would you agree there's tremendous value in looking at how you've created your relationship experiences up to this point?

You have the power to control how your relationships go and, ultimately, how your life goes. How you perceive your past, present, and future relationships make it so. Perception makes your reality. If you let go of the need to (*a*) be right, (*b*) be hurt, (*c*) blame, (*d*) harm, and (*e*) convince, then it provides something else: possibility. There is a possibility your relationships can unfold differently from this point forward; it could be how your heart has been aching for it to unfold. Are you willing to become more responsible to have the relationship you've always wanted?

And We're Off...

We have a saying in coaching that "we're being called forth." Being called forth is an invitation to explore, face the discomfort, and stand in the face of your resistance. This chapter is meant to call you forth in ways you may not be accustomed to, and will probably feel uncomfortable. Without choosing to be called forth, you're almost sure to repeat your past mistakes and relationship blunders. In every relationship, you've created an agreement between yourself and another person. You chose them. If you're not getting what you want, then choose differently. Let's get started.

I invite you to be open and willing and to explore how taking responsibility for your failed relationships will free you to create something new. You could create the relationship you've always wanted, dreamed of, and desired—fairytale shit—for real. Relationships are incredibly complicated, with many variables affecting how you experience and impact your partners.

Take 100 percent responsibility for your relationships. There are situations where a person has been abused, traumatized, abandoned, and many other terrible scenarios. If that describes you, then my heart goes out to you. Don't take responsibility for what happened but take responsibility for how you responded. In any situation, your power, even in a powerless situation, is how you respond, relate, and adapt to your circumstances. It's critical to make this vital distinction.

There are many ways that you can be in and approach your relationships. Noticing who you are in all areas of life, especially in your relationships, has the power to fundamentally alter your experiences. I've found through (*a*) my training, (*b*) working with my clients, (*c*) my marriage, and (*d*) the experience from my relationships that understanding who I'm being in creating these individual relationships is the key to making them successful.

Choosing to Be

What do I mean by **being**? Your being is the essence of who you are —period. Your being isn't what you do but who you are. Most of us get a little lost in the weeds when it comes to understanding our being. It's easy to get wrapped up in what you do to describe yourself. You may have become lost, bitter, and exhausted just to be.

Take a moment. Take a few deep breaths and attempt to clear your mind and just be. There is no other you on earth. You're unique and have gifts to share by that virtue alone. Those gifts aren't generated from what you do but by who you are, simply by being yourself.

During coach training, I was asked to choose my personal-growth journey. It was a journey of intense self-realization and exploration and an incredibly challenging and rewarding life experience. I was reintroduced to myself—who I am—by simply being me. That sounds funny, but it's true. The unique version of me has gifts of love, adventure, and brilliance to share with a partner while also being a fuller expression of who I was created to be. I got to meet that guy again.

None of who I was being was tied to accomplishments, the letters following my name, the money in my account, or my beautiful, successful partner. It fascinated me that this awareness opened the door to more possibilities. Being myself without performing or acting like who society wanted me to be, I could access levels of power and joy I'd never experienced. If you want to learn more about being, check out "ontology." It's the branch of metaphysics that deals with the nature of our being. It can be a bit of a mind-bender, but this knowledge provides access to a new way of approaching your life and relationships. This approach will give you access to the type of relationships you want. I'm not here to drag you into a philosophy lesson, but it is essential to know the following phrases and terminology:

- ◆ **We be** means simply being who you are when you're free.
- ◆ **We do** means you create and achieve, but this isn't who you are.
- ◆ **Doing is not being** means you aren't what you do or achieve.
- ◆ **We are being while we are doing** means you have a choice of who you choose to be while creating and achieving.
- ◆ **We can choose who we are** means you always have a choice in how you (*a*) perceive, (*b*) interact with, and (*c*) experience your life and relationships.

There are fundamentally two places you can choose to be regarding your relationships. You can be victimized by (*a*) your relationships, (*b*) your partners, (*c*) the past, (*d*) what was said or not said, and (*e*) a host of other factors, or **you can be responsible for those relationships**. Most of us are a combination of victimized and responsible. Sometimes you may be more responsible than victimized. At other times, you may be more victimized than responsible. This is the ebb and flow of a relationship as you're challenged and rewarded in your experience. In a relationship, you can either choose to be victimized or be responsible for it. I want to make sure you understand how important it is to make that distinction.

This is crucially important for you to understand. Being a victim is a choice. Being responsible is a choice. It will take a daily practice to be intentional about who you're being and repeatedly choose who you want to be during your quest **for love** or your quest **in love**. Be sure you understand and accept this. We're discussing a new way to access power and love in your relationships. This isn't the only way, but it's an effective way, a way that works.

It will take effort, but it will be worth it. The level of freedom you'll experience once you become responsible for your relationships will give you access to levels of joy and ease you've never experienced. It will require practice because you've probably never taken 100 percent responsibility for your relationships at this level. Most people don't. When it comes to this, most people are clueless. Kelly certainly was.

Committed to Complaining

Kelly was so angry when she got on the phone with me. She ranted for ten minutes. Kelly's friend referred her to me, so she reached out to discuss some of her relationship challenges. I knew about Kelly through our social circle. From all outward appearances, she had her shit together. She had a well-paying job and drove a nice car. Kelly had a great smile and a wonderful laugh. She was intellectually brilliant and presented herself well.

After I listened to her complain about everything her partner was doing—from the uncapped toothpaste tube to the cigarette ashes on the porch to all the ways her partner wasn't loving and honoring her—I finally interrupted, "Hey, what do you want from our conversation?"

"What do you mean?" she asked.

I said, "You've been complaining about your partner for ten minutes straight, and I can't get a word in. So what do you want from me or this?

Did you call just to complain? If that's helpful, great, but how will it change anything?"

Kelly was silent. She needed to vent. But in the end, who cares?

I was curious about what she wanted—what she **truly** wanted—not what she didn't want. "Why are you staying in this relationship if it doesn't meet your needs?" I asked.

Deflecting the question, she began complaining about her partner again.

"Are you open to answering the question I asked?" I interrupted.

She didn't answer my question because she was more committed to making her partner wrong than being responsible for creating the relationships she wanted. Being responsible meant it was time to stop pointing the finger at her partner and begin pointing it at herself. Kelly couldn't communicate what she wanted or why she stayed in a relationship that wasn't working. In this way, she got to remain a victim of her partner's behavior and the uncapped tube of toothpaste he left behind daily,

Her complaints were simply a symptom of not being loved and honored in a way that made a difference. Kelly's partner may have been trying the best way he knew how, but it wasn't making a difference. Both of them probably weren't getting what they wanted or needed.

We spent a few more minutes on the phone and discussed logistics. She didn't want to work with me, work on herself, or become responsible for her relationships. I'm never attached to someone's choice to work with me, but I often wonder how their results would be different without structure. One of the greatest benefits of working with a coach is the structure it provides. Part of that structure is engaging in weekly sessions to discover what you genuinely want. A coach inspires you to spark your curiosity about what you want and why you want it. Then you both uncover the circumstances that can get in between you and the desired outcome. Being accountable to someone there to push you toward your goals and dreams is, easily, one of the most uncomfortable yet proven ways to achieve what you want. Who would possibly say no to that?

Kelly writes a few whiny posts portraying herself as the victim on my social media wall now and then. She's more committed to wanting and wishing she had the relationship she desires rather than investing, doing the work, and creating it. We'll discuss "wanting" much more in Chapter 15. Kelly couldn't overcome her victim mentality and continues to make that her experience of a relationship.

The energy she puts into being right about being wrong could be spent creating an authentic, loving partnership.

Victim

Everything happens to the victim. They are wronged, and others are to blame. If you're the victim, you get to be righteous when you insist on being right about being wronged, and relationships happen to you. There is fear waiting for the next disaster to occur in your love life that has you stuck in a protective, defensive posture.

You build a wall of protection to guard your heart. Victims create drama to help them predict their future. It's a form of self-sabotage because the victim will create the reality they desperately want to avoid.

Since the unknown is so uncomfortable, a victim will disrupt the present to predict the future. Victims will start a fight over something petty and then need their partner to reaffirm and prove their love. This creates a predictable, go-away-and-come-here cycle. The victim almost unknowingly creates this cycle and sadly enjoys it. Victims focus on what could go wrong. Victims are reactive and, well, victim-y.

Your partner is the asshole. Wait—"**All men** are assholes!" "Women are too needy and emotional." "Why are all the good ones taken?" "At my age, everyone has baggage. So what's the point in believing I can get what I want?" "If they would only (fill in the victim-y blank), then I could (fill in the victim-y blank)." It's a powerless way to be in relationships. You're always at the mercy of everyone and everything else. You're a victim.

You may ask, "How do you expect me not to be a victim when all this is happening?" All types of things can victimize us. Of course, the obvious horrible situations occur in abusive relationships. These circumstances are unacceptable. You're not responsible for them, but you're responsible for leaving them. Please do so.

I'm pointing to the small, daily irritations we allow to victimize us in our relationships. Let's use Kelly as an example. She remained victimized by her partner

◆ Being too tired to pay her the attention she wants
◆ Not responding fast enough to a text message
◆ Leaving the house without giving her a hug

- Leaving cigarette ashes on the porch
- Leaving dirty laundry on the floor, and
- Leaving behind his uncapped tube of toothpaste.

The list could go on but take note of your favorite ways to be right about being wronged. Daily irritations add up and will impact the experience you have in relationships. So be responsible for them. Kelly isn't wrong about how she feels, but she can become responsible for her feelings to create something different with her partner.

But Wait, There's More

If it's happening in your relationships, it's probably happening in other facets of your life. Look at your career, family, and finances, then notice who you're being. Where else are you being a victim? Do you have a preoccupation with someone's action or inaction at work? Do you assess and keep score of who is and isn't doing what they're supposed to do?

Are you the odd one out of your family who constantly draws criticism and negativity? Remember your earliest relationships were the ones you had with your (genetic or chosen) family. We pick up and learn how to be in relationships from there. It's your ground zero for growing up to become a victim.

The characteristics of victims include:
- Being reactive (They react to someone or something else versus creating a relationship.)
- Blaming others (They point the finger outward when it comes to all of life's problems.)
- Needing external validation (They must always earn their worth and love.)
- Feeling powerless (They feel no sense of their power to create their experience.)
- Lacking responsibility (They feel that everything is everyone else's fault.)
- Creating drama (They gossip because they seek others to validate their claims.)
- Living in repetitive patterns of discontent (They boohoo everywhere.)

◆ Avoiding risk. (They'd rather be comfortable complaining about not having the relationship they want, versus becoming uncomfortable to create it.)

Get Your Shit Together

Choosing to be responsible is like opening a doorway to your personal power. You gain control over how you experience relationships regardless of what's happening in them. You're the creator of your happiness, joy, and love. Being responsible in a relationship means looking inward first toward whatever you're facing. What does that look like? Only after you become responsible for yourself can you look to your partner and your relationship. So how do you become responsible? Choose it. Responsibility is a choice that requires an intentional way of being. It's a reinvention and a new beginning in how you approach, experience, and end relationships.

When you're responsible, you're not affected by your thoughts, feelings, or sensations in your body. You're simply aware of what is and what you must do. My coach is an expert at reminding me of this fact. After listening to me vent, ramble, or provide evidence as to why I can't have everything I want, he'll ask a simple yet powerful question. I'll ask you the same question.

So Now What?

You likely have a set of beliefs about how relationships should be. Despite how you've experienced them or how you think they will be, ask yourself, "So now what?" Whether it's the stories you've made up about (*a*) your partner, (*b*) the lack of having a partner, or (*c*) the difficulty you've experienced while trying to find one, ask yourself again, "So now what?" What will you do in the face of not having the relationship you want? Most importantly, **who will you be?** This is the moment to choose; it's the time to take a different action. If you use this moment to make the same choice, you'll get the same results as you've always got. You have a decision to make. What identifies a victim mindset in life and relationships is the perspective that you don't have control over what's happening. The opportunity is to become responsible for being the victim in your relationships.

Use the following tips to take a thorough inventory of what you can be responsible for in your relationships:

◆ Notice your behavioral patterns and what triggers you.

Gaining knowledge of your patterns and triggers is your work, not the work of your current or future partner. If you're currently in a relationship, bring this conversation up with your partner. Say, "Hey, when you say or do this, I make it mean this. I know it's not the truth, but when I get triggered (scared), this is what's going on inside me."

◆ Start a conversation in a way that creates a safe dialogue with your partner.

It's incredibly supportive to have someone partner with you so you can be held accountable for portraying yourself as a victim. If your partner is willing, they'll also have an opportunity to be held responsible, portraying themselves as a victim. Communicating this way allows you both to become closer and more loving toward each other. We all have an inner victim because it's a part of our survival mechanism, but we need to be less attached to it.

◆ Practice being responsible with your thoughts, speech, and actions.

In the beginning, this will be like flexing a weak muscle. If you're intentional and responsible, miraculous things will happen over time. You'll start to pause before thinking, speaking, and acting like a victim.

People who use this introspection to take responsibility for intentional thought, speech, and actions move from being victims to victors. The characteristics of victors include being:

◆ Proactive (You create your experience of your life and relationships.)
◆ Powerful (You are a creator and clear about what you want.)
◆ Forgiving (You forgive others and move on.)
◆ Accountable (You're accountable for your actions, thoughts, and words.).
◆ Vulnerable (You both seek and ask for support.).

◆ Open (You are open to giving and receiving feedback).

◆ Explorational (You are curious and willing to get uncomfortable), and

◆ Willing to take upside risks (You'll get outside your comfort zone to get what you want).

So what's it going to be? Will you be a victim of circumstances and blame everyone else in your relationships? Or will you take 100 percent responsibility for your role? Choose now. Face the discomfort of getting outside your comfort zone. Maybe, just maybe—you'll create the relationship you've always wanted. Finally, a relationship that doesn't suck.

CHAPTER FOUR

IDENTIFICATION OF PATTERNS

> Love isn't finding a perfect person. It's seeing an imperfect person perfectly.
>
> - Sam Keen, *To Love and Be Loved*

"Well, what can you see about your patterns?"

"What do you mean?" Jane asked as I sensed discomfort in her voice.

"This is your third relationship that's ended this way, right?" I asked, curious.

"Yes."

"What do you notice? Can you see anything pointing to why this continues to happen for you?"

I sensed a bit more discomfort from Jane. We were going to start poking the bear and pouring salt in the wound, then twisting a thorn in its side. As we examined her relationship patterns and explored where and how she could be responsible for her part, there was more discomfort, resistance, and yet willingness because Jane desperately wanted to experience her relationships differently.

My clients tend to not like exploring their patterns because it requires an honest interpretation of their role in their relationship breakdowns. It's uncomfortable because the focus and spotlight are removed from someone else so they can start taking responsibility. Do you notice a sudden stirring of resistance? That's good because it proves there is a piece of you being transformed by reading this book—the work that's beginning the journey to accepting responsibility.

One of the most potent and impactful choices you'll make while reading this book is to become responsible for your shit. Guess what? You won't like it, and that's okay. Allow yourself to be honest, open, and willing in your process. Too often in relationships, someone plays the victim—winning the Oscar® for having been wronged in the relationship. Unfortunately, this won't make any difference, so knock it off. We're not playing a game where someone wins, and another loses. We're playing a game where both win and get the reward.

Taking responsibility for your relationships and identifying your patterns will provide you with a road map. You'll see where you need to do internal work to overcome challenges and seize the opportunities available to create a new way to be in relationships. If you want a new relationship experience, it will take busting up some old stuff. Do you notice when your behaviors or your current/future partner's behaviors are not aligned with who you want to be or who you want to be with?

Becoming an observer of your patterns in a relationship will provide the opportunity to interrupt it. This level of observation is important for you because you'll:

◆ Notice a predictable pattern.
◆ Become responsible for the pattern.
◆ Have the ability to interrupt the pattern.
◆ Gain access to the power of making a different choice.
◆ Communicate your pattern clearly.
◆ You will create different results.

This will be an ongoing practice for you while you're actively in and creating relationships.

The practice of interrupting your predictable patterns will be easier with time and repetition, similar to flexing a weak muscle. Think of it as a membership to the "awareness gym," where you'll lift awareness weights and run on the responsibility treadmill. The more you flex and exercise these muscles over time, the stronger, bigger, and more powerful they'll become.

Teaching an Old Dog

Patterns are a repetition of behavior and who you're being; repetition is how you do things and who you are in situations. Aside from your relationship, look at a part of your day. For example, look at your morning routine. What patterns do you notice? Do you wake up at a certain time? Do you drink your coffee, tea, or water right away or wait? Do you shower? Do you use the same soap and shampoo? How about your oral hygiene? Do you brush your teeth after you shower or before? Do you floss? You had better be flossing. If not, then why don't you floss? Is it the time required? You don't like doing it? Does it hurt and make your gums bleed? Is it something you know you should be doing but don't?

We're habitual creatures and our habits live inside our patterns of behavior and being. I assert that you have a particular way of creating your relationships. I also assert that you show up for and "be" in relationships in a specific way. Open yourself up to exploring what patterns serve you and which ones do not. Become curious about what you're willing to transform about yourself to create the relationships you want. When one is triggered, scared, or on the verge of creating new outcomes, old patterns become a respite for the uneasiness of being outside one's comfort zone.

Jane, another one of my rock-star clients, noticed a particular pattern around her requests for intimacy. Jane is one of the smartest women I know. She has an alphabet soup of letters after her name to demonstrate to the world the number of degrees and certifications she's earned. These letters declare her brilliance to all who see her signature line. One of our early conversations while working together inspired this chapter's opening.

We discovered a distinguishable pattern, a specific form of sabotage Jane used. She would lure her partner in, and once she had a committed relationship with that partner, she'd unknowingly push her away. It was a game of come here, now go away. She excelled at this game and always won; however, she lost because she wanted a girlfriend, but ended up alone time and time again. Jane was ready to break up her non-serving patterns.

Jane and I began identifying her patterns. We paid particular attention to common themes surrounding how her relationships unfold and who she becomes as the relationship progresses. This was a gold mine of information and provided her with an opportunity to choose something different. Jane and I worked through a few sessions and created some awareness practices for when her come-here-now-go-away mechanism started to activate. Ultimately, she discovered it was based on fear. She feared the woman would leave her anyway, so why not cut to the chase and run her off?

Jane was ready to take responsibility for this in her next relationship. She created the opportunity to share her pattern with her partner and take action to mitigate its effects. She explored what worked for her and her partner when her runaway patterns inevitably appeared.

As I was writing this book, I reached out to her to see how things were going. She's currently in a relationship with a woman and is very excited about being with her. What's remarkable is that she brought this mechanism to her partner and shared it with her. By discussing her relationship pattern, she opened up a ton of intimacy. This included identifying (*a*) what it is (fear), (*b*) why it exists (to create a predictable experience to lessen the fear), and (*c*) actions to take when it gets activated (sharing it). She had positive results because she created awareness. She acted and remained responsible for herself.

Another client of mine, James, resisted exploring this awareness of behavioral patterns for himself. He was forever the victim, and it was nearly impossible for James to take complete responsibility for his interpretation and experience of relationships. James was resistant to the possibility that any of his relationships could be blamed on him. His inability to be honest with himself and his resistance to taking responsibility for his failed relationships are typical responses I often encounter.

Looking at yourself in this manner is uncomfortable, but so is the consequence of not looking. The discomfort of looking or not looking at your gaps will pass; however, only looking at these gaps and doing the internal work to address the source of pain will create a new relationship experience. If honestly looking at your patterns will suck, either way, you might as well suck in the direction of the relationship you want.

James's pattern also had to do with intimacy (basically, the lack of it). He would go through the motions but not allow anyone or anything in. He acted like a boyfriend and did all the right things but never truly allowed himself to be vulnerable, open, and curious. Repeatedly, his partners commonly requested this vulnerability, openness, and curiosity and complained about the lack of it. They wanted more of James's heart and emotion, but he was like an emotional robot. He would get involved in relationships with partners who needed a high sense of emotional intelligence and connection—a total mismatch.

In the early stages of his relationships, James's pattern was to hide behind humor and great looks. When his partners wanted more from him emotionally, he would shut down. Opening up this way was threatening for James, so he would shut down and go through the motions.

We created some practices for James to begin to open his heart and mouth to share what was going on in his brilliant mind and colossal heart with his partner. On our weekly calls, he would report not having completed any of the practices he created. Some circumstances or issues prevented him from talking to his partner in a meaningful way. It's not that there is anything wrong with this, but nothing was changing. He simply wasn't ready to try anything new and get a different result. Although this resistance came at a cost, he was fine with how he was.

James and his partner ended their relationship, and he missed the remainder of his calls with me. He disappeared. The call forth for him to share himself was too great of a risk, so he lost his relationship with his partner and sabotaged the one he had with his coach. Whatever was feeding his pattern was undoubtedly not serving his greater interests in finding a partner. It was too great of a request for James to (a) interrupt the pattern of how he chose women to date, (b) change who he was while in a relationship, and (c) take more responsibility for himself. So he got the same result he always has, loneliness.

Science Stuff

If you care about science stuff, then read this section. There's a physiological component to interrupting your patterns. Understanding this will support you as you break up your patterns to create a new and lasting approach to building relationships. Simply put, our brains are lazy—super lazy. Some may call it maximizing efficiency, but it looks for the shortest, least energy-expending process possible. Think of it as the foundation of your patterns in a relationship. How many times have you observed the **here-we-go-again** phenomena inside your relationship? It's almost as if you've been trained to see what you've been seeing. For example, think of how you immediately interpret the meaning when your partner looks at you in a certain way or takes a certain amount of time to respond to your text or your bid for their attention. All these interpretations are inside patterns, and some can be destructive.

So let's discuss an important concept; it's known as priming. When you've been exposed over and over to a specific stimulus, your brain begins to prime your response. The lazy brain primes itself to interpret a subsequent stimulus with the same response even when it's not warranted. So how does this play out in a relationship? Ah, let's go on some dates.

This is so prevalent in dating. It's painfully prevalent. As I work with my single clients, we typically discuss how (1) terrible dates have been, (2) online dating is full of weirdos or people with baggage, and (3) weekday dates are going to suck. Many of my clients have primed themselves going into these dates and situations. Guess what? The dates are terrible, the people they attract are weirdos or have baggage, and their weekday dates suck. It's like priming almost predicts the future. If you look for it, you'll find it and create it.

Discover where your patterns are reinforced as a result of how you've been primed to view relationships. Begin to create a new relationship with how you interpret the experience of your relationships. Start by using a few of these tactics:

- Get clear about what you want. (What do you want to experience?)
- Create a relationship with your brain and its internal processing and interpretation. (Step outside yourself, get out of the weeds, and elevate.)
- Notice if you're getting what you want. (You may be and yet have been primed to not see it or be with it.)
- Check yourself and adjust accordingly. (What do you notice about yourself and your patterns that you can change?)

How It Goes

Ready to identify your patterns in relationships? I will share a few questions to support you as you uncover your patterns and stimulate some thought. Your awareness will be key. The ability to interrupt a predictable pattern that doesn't serve you will pay dividends. Here are some questions to help you discover your relationship patterns:

- Where do you meet your partners?
- What are the first few interactions like?

- ◆ How do you feel?
- ◆ What are you excited/nervous about?
- ◆ Do you say or do anything inauthentic?
- ◆ Are you anything other than yourself?
- ◆ When you commit, do you truly do it?
- ◆ When do you get physically active?
- ◆ What happens at the first hint of disagreement?
- ◆ What expectations go unmet?
- ◆ Does resentment, confusion, and fear build?
- ◆ What triggers your resentment, confusion, or fear?
- ◆ Do you start to pull away or lean in all the way? (Then what happens? What happens after that?)
- ◆ When does your heart begin to break?
- ◆ When do you realize that your partner is/isn't the one for you?
- ◆ When does the relationship end?

Create the Value

With practice, you'll find a ton of value in being an excellent observer of yourself. Whether you're in a relationship, seeking one, or actively trying to get out of one, identifying your predictable patterns will provide access to power and possibility. It's easy to slip back into old, **convenient patterns,** so consider this a journey rather than a destination.

Become an observer of yourself in a partnership with your current or future person. This will require you to have a vulnerable conversation aloud about (*a*) sharing the value of this self-awareness, (*b*) what you'll both commit to, and (*c*) what action you'll take to interrupt the pattern when it shows up again—because it will.

Dan, one of my clients, shared an amazing story that provides a perfect example of what interrupting a pattern looks like. Dan is in his late forties, a successful entrepreneur, semi-retired after selling his business, and in a new relationship. He thought this might be the one, but he never arrived at the point of being fully committed while taking complete responsibility for himself in a relationship.

One night, he was cooking dinner for his girlfriend. He shared how excited he was to cook for her and try a new recipe. It was a chicken dish with a lot of Indian spices— something new and different for him. When his partner arrived, she stood next to him in the kitchen and asked him about the recipe and the process. Her response was, "Wow, that's a lot of spice."

Dan noticed that he immediately went into a defensive posture. He shared that he felt a bit insecure while making this new recipe because he wasn't sure how it would turn out and whether or not his girlfriend would like it. Dan's thoughts primed his response to be defensive. "I'm going to fuck this up. It's not going to be good. She won't like it. I'm going to ruin dinner."

So his girlfriend's comment was primed through the context of Dan screwing up dinner. Dan noticed this and immediately took responsibility; then, he put it on loudspeaker. He shared what was coming up for him. From his default reaction, Dan would have shut down, got quiet, and began growing resentment toward his girlfriend. Instead, he recognized this and said, "Hey, when you said there was a lot of spice, I made it mean that I'm ruining dinner, and you won't like it."

His girlfriend shared, "I'm super excited about how spicy this meal will be because I've been craving some spicy food,"

Dan avoided a night of resentment, shame, and being right about being wronged. By sharing what was going on through his primed filter, he interrupted his pattern and made himself vulnerable. We celebrated this as a win for him. Dinner went well, and his actions and vulnerability created deeper levels of intimacy with his girlfriend. They now have the space to say whatever they need to say to be present, loving, and empowered.

If this level of vulnerability and connection cannot be created with your partner, then ask yourself if this is your person. This can be an uncomfortable, awkward, and scary place for some. Your partner will likely react from their (default) pattern and primed responses. This is normal.

For example, your partner may respond by saying, "Everything is fine. Why do we have to talk about this?" This is a typical response from a person who isn't connected to the significance of the upcoming breakdown of the relationship. Is everything really fine? Is this person willing to explore with their partner and begin the process of resolving the conflict?

Keep leaning into the conversation with them. Keep practicing **with** them and not **at** them. Don't allow your pattern to use this awareness as a weapon and break down communication further. When created in partnership, this is one of the most valuable tools that you'll have to stop your relationships from sucking.

CHAPTER FIVE

LETTING GO: DROP YOUR RIGHTEOUSNESS

> "Forget what hurt you in the past, but never forget what it taught you."
> - Shannon Alder

Righteousness in your relationship journey is simply choosing to be right. It's not wrong to be right; however, I assert that your **rightness** gets in the way of creating a new and better relationship. Seek to (*a*) understand what happened, (*b*) get the gold from the lessons, (*c*) let go of the past, and (*d*) create your future.

"I'll never find love," Joyce shared in a sharp, emotionally distraught tone. "How do you know?" I asked. It's a simple question, and if you take a moment to answer it, it's a powerful answer to discover.

How could she possibly know? She was living as if she knew her future outcome. Could that understanding, that righteousness, ultimately create that future outcome? I would say yes. Your mindset and heart-set can directly impact your future and what you believe is possible. We had the opportunity to help Joyce break down the context regarding her possibility of ever finding love. This opportunity required us to start with Joyce's willingness to overcome a bullshit mindset. Like Joyce, if you're constantly looking for why you can't have what you want, then the Universe will grant you exactly that. The Universe loves you and wants to give you what you ask for. So ask for what you truly want and not for what you don't want.

One of the primary reasons your relationships suck is because you continue dragging the past into them. A comforting feeling comes from being right or being a victim and not taking responsibility for how you currently experience your relationship. You're comfortable in your familiar misery. Someone has wronged you, and you get to be righteous about it. Maybe your ex was an asshole or too needy (or several other reasons to rationalize how your ex was wrong), so you get to be right. Relationships can bring up horrible situations which involve abuse, addiction, trauma, shame, and neglect. Although it's critical to get the support to handle those instances properly, I'm not referring to these situations. Why aren't you letting go of the petty hurt and blame? Isn't it time to open yourself up to healing and new possibilities?

After the dust has settled from your heartbreak (either from another failed relationship or after not finding **the one**), it's time to release your past once you're ready. You may wonder what that means. It means that you must confront the past as an opportunity to release all the burdensome energy that holds you, your heart, and the possibility of love as hostages. This energy is insidious because it festers. So it must go.

This negative energy is still impacting you today. All the old thoughts, feelings, and body sensations are getting in the way of the new experience you want to create. Not letting go of the past creates predictable patterns in your current and future relationships. Yes, the past will repeat itself until you learn to release yourself from it. I'm not suggesting for a moment that you forget the past or the lessons that you've learned. I suggest you allow the past to be just the past once the energy surrounding past events has cleared. That's it. No judgment. It simply **is** the past. You might even begin to get some gold out of your heartbreaking experiences.

Clean Slate

The goal is to have no energy around what comes up. The past simply is the past. Your past relationships are there to teach you without defining you. For example, if a memory of a specific conversation comes up that you and your ex-partner had, there is no longer any energy behind it. It just was. You notice who you were, who your partner was, what was said, and what wasn't said. There is no judgment or feelings. It's simply a memory.

If this sounds as possible to you as walking on the sun, then it confirms the need for you to let go. Why are you holding onto negative beliefs and experiences so tightly? Do you need to be right? Do you want to punish your past partners or even yourself—I mean—how could you, after all? Permit yourself to (a) let it go, (b) forgive, and (c) move on. What have you got to lose? If forgiving and releasing hasn't been a practice of yours or an experience that you're familiar with, then are you willing to dig in? Are you ready to explore the possibility of letting go of the past hurt to clear out your negative beliefs and create the shift that you've wanted—the shift in how you both give and receive love?

Letting go creates a fresh foundation for everything new and different you'll create after your heartbreak. All my clients do a **letting go** exercise at some point in our coaching relationship. Usually, it happens within the first few sessions as it becomes painfully clear that they're still holding on to what they need to release. Letting go is an opportunity to become clear, present, responsible, and empowered about what's next. Letting go is a gradual evolution; it's never a one-and-done exercise. The process is a journey and not a destination. You'll need to let go over and over again to create something different in your relationships. Old feelings, thoughts, and body sensations will sometimes rise unexpectedly. Be responsible and do some internal work to release this energy. Notice it, name it, and get in action to get the support you need. Become responsible.

When it Hit Me

I was on a tough call with one of my clients, Bill. He was discussing his recent breakup, which was emotionally brutal. Bill was an amazing, caring, loving, but sometimes brash business owner. He was vulnerably sharing with me the story of his failed relationship. He sobbed over what had happened and what could've been. He was in the depths of his heartbreak, and it was a compelling client call. Suddenly, out of nowhere, intense emotion welled up inside me too. It was so intense that I had to pause and ask for a moment. I began sobbing too. I felt out of control of my emotions, and the emotional reaction came out of nowhere. I'm trained not to take on my client's energy, but somehow this sneaked in.

Feelings from my previous relationship came up. And they came up **strong**. All the old feelings, the sadness about how it ended, and the regret flooded back like an oncoming tsunami. At the time, I was in my forever relationship with the woman of my dreams and soon-to-be-married. Why did these thoughts, feelings, and body sensations come up for my ex? I noticed how I immediately judged my ex. I also judged myself for having these feelings so suddenly. My past came back. It reminded me that I was still holding on to something.

My client graciously gave me a few minutes to compose myself. At that moment, it surprised me, and I said, "Holy shit, where did this come from?" The experience provided valuable awareness for myself and my client. Letting go is a journey and not a destination. I knew I had more work to do, so I did. Bill and I continued our call together and created actions for moving toward what both of us were creating in our relationship experiences. It was a beautiful moment that started some cool intimacy between us. As a result of this exchange, Bill learned through firsthand experience that letting go is a gradual process. He wanted the quick fix to make it go away and numb his pain and heartbreak.

Holding on and going numb leads many of us into another relationship too soon. We might drink, eat, sleep, do drugs, or numb ourselves with sex, porn, or another distraction. It's a survival response. It's okay to process heartbreak this way. I'm not judging, but ask yourself if it's serving you - honestly.

You're Going to Resist This

Letting go is the ultimate act of forgiveness, and you'll resist it. The resistance protects you. It protects you from (a) creating something new, (b) stepping outside your comfort zone, and (c) letting you face your challenges, including what they are and are not. It requires confronting the hurt and negative beliefs. It's an opportunity to experience a different kind of relationship from this day forward. I invite you to push past your resistance and do whatever it takes to release the past. Release the power and energy it has over you.

You may ask, "Great, but how?" The rest of this chapter is devoted to answering that question. Yes, this is work, but remember that different results require different actions.

Judgment Day

Welcome to the turning point. This is the day when you begin creating your new experience of relationships. Throughout your life, you have gathered evidence about how you think, believe, and feel relationships should be. We all do it. You probably watched your parents or parent navigate through their relationships as a young child. So you began collecting images and experiences that created your relationship paradigm. On the big screen, love stories in novels or romantic comedies (romcoms) also shape and define how you think and feel about relationships.

Begin to observe your relationship patterns (specifically). This observation is essential so you can start identifying the gaps (and what's in them) and gaining new awareness to get into (further and probably uncomfortable) action.

Think back to your earliest memory about what being in a relationship meant. Then answer the questions below. I invite you to approach this as a journaling exercise. You can also just ponder these questions if you would like, but my clients and my experience have taught me that healing or catharsis happens through writing.

Grab a notebook, block out some time in your schedule, and get to work by answering the following questions:

- ◆ Where did you learn how to be in a relationship?
- ◆ From whom or what? (Family, friends, the movies, etc.)
- ◆ Did they have the relationship that you wanted?
- ◆ How did that relationship work out for them or you?
- ◆ What did you have to do to make it work?
- ◆ Who did you have to be to make it work?
- ◆ What jeopardized the relationship?
- ◆ What made it successful?
- ◆ Was there tragedy, danger, or misfortune tied to the relationship?
- ◆ Did this relationship repeat another's or your pattern?

Take time to explore where you formed your earliest beliefs about relationships. Consider how influential these memories were in creating your expectations of how relationships should be. You formulated judgments, assessments, and an understanding of your relationship's foundation from these memories. It's time to uncover it. If it's built on a shaky foundation, everything you've built until this point or will build in the future will never be stable. This phenomenon is essential to note and get clear about. Seek clarity and understanding about what influences shaped your beliefs and feelings about how relationships **should be**.

You're going to create a judgment day. Get your calendar right now. Schedule a day. Put this book down and schedule it. Write "Letting Go Day" in your calendar and give yourself at least a few hours.

This may seem overwhelming, and you'll resist. I assure you, on the other side, completing this exercise is an essential lesson about your relationship patterns. Connect with a loved one who understands what you're about to challenge yourself to do. Ask to lean on them for support as you work through the process. I also highly encourage you to create a system of accountability to complete this step because you'll absolutely resist it.

As a part of Letting Go Day, I highly suggest you do this as a five-part writing exercise. It may seem like a big dramatic deal, but I know you got this. While keeping your goals in mind, you love yourself in a way you may have never loved yourself before. The goal is to create **the love of your life!**

Part I

Write down the names of all your past and current relationships and make a list that includes the following people:

- ◆ Partners
- ◆ Friends
- ◆ Parents/family
- ◆ Crushes
- ◆ High school sweethearts
- ◆ All the people you've loved

Part II

Write down all your romantic relationships. You may have positive, negative, and indifferent judgments about these people. Write all of it. Get it out of your head and onto the paper. Doing this will make you feel confronted, and that's the point. Permit yourself not to be elevated or enlightened at this moment. Get your rawness out on paper. Keep this in a safe place so those you love never find it. I'm sure you can imagine why.

As you move through this, behavioral patterns will begin to emerge. These patterns, beliefs, and judgments are the road map to your internal work. It's the flashlight shining a new awareness and an opportunity on how you create relationships. This is the call forth and the time for you to (*a*) become responsible, (*b*) let go, and (*c*) create what you want.

Part III

In an area under the section where you wrote your judgments, identify the behavioral patterns you notice. Here are some examples:

◆ Codependent
◆ Independent
◆ Stubborn
◆ Care-free
◆ Loving
◆ Manipulative
◆ Effortless

Spend as much time as you need to decipher your patterns from the lists you create. Get to the essence of the experience from that relationship. Give it a name or a phrase and circle it. Again, take another moment to notice the patterns and reflect on everything you've circled. What do you notice?

For example, in familial relationships, your behavior often resembles that of a fixer. You attempt to fix, manage, and control others' feelings. Sometimes you make others feel good at the expense of your well-being.

In romantic relationships, you may notice stubbornness and rigidity in what you allow. Or you may have expectations about how your partner must show up in relationships. Do you let them be themselves? Or do you have a belief about how you feel they should show up?

Spend time carefully picking out the clues regarding how your relationships have gone. I promise there will be some genuine gold nuggets for you. Be willing to pick up that gold and learn from it. Use it to act differently. If you want to know how you create relationships, then you will. This is the start of experiencing your relationships differently.

Part IV

This part may sting a bit, but it's time to identify your role in the relationship. This isn't to let your previous partners off the hook for any mistreatment. Consider it as owning your stuff and an actual act of self-love. It's also an act of empowerment. After all, you're reading this book. They aren't. They're on their path. At some point, perhaps sharing what you learn from this book would be a loving act, but let's keep the focus on you for now.

Taking responsibility gives you access to power. You can take responsibility for your part in having bad, unfulfilled relationships. Once you become responsible for your part, you'll have greater access to choosing new actions and ways of being in your relationships so they can become exciting, loving, and fulfilling. The past doesn't have to impact your present and future decisions, actions, and beliefs. You're finally free.

Write down what part of the experience of your relationships you can honestly own as your role. What can you be responsible for? For example, I can acknowledge that I manipulated my partners with feelings of guilt when they would leave me to go out with friends.

There is an opportunity in the future to explore what you've learned about yourself with a coach. Your new awareness is the gold. However, awareness without action won't create the results that you want. A coach will support you as you take action amidst your discomfort, confusion, and lack of willingness. Your coach is your partner in creating lasting change.

Presents!

What was the gift for you as you went through this exercise? Did you do it? If yes, then congratulations! You've loved yourself in a way that you likely haven't before. This level of deep introspection, digging up the yuck, and taking responsibility for it is courageous—incredibly courageous.

If you read through the exercise but didn't do the writing, then take a moment and notice what's in your space right now. Ask yourself the following questions:

- Are you feeling like you shouldn't have to do this?
- Is there no value in doing this?
- Do you think everything will just fix itself over time?
- Seriously look at your resistance. It's completely fine. Remember, I gave you a heads-up that you'd resist. You don't necessarily have to do this work this way. You simply may not be ready yet. If you did it, then list what this experience has given you. After, ask yourself the following questions:
- Are you willing to go deeper?
- What action will you take with your new awareness?
- What support do you need to create results?
- How committed are you to creating new relationship results?

Are You Clean?

The slate has been cleaned. The past is the past, and you now have access to the future you've been yearning to enjoy. Remember, your old mindset and patterns will return. Notice them and see what you can be responsible for. Then choose to act in alignment with the relationship outcomes that you want now. This won't be easy. You'll make mistakes as you keep striving for what you want.

Acknowledge your misstep and the backslide. Be curious about what's going on with you emotionally, spiritually, mentally, and physically. Where did or didn't you listen to your intuition, ease up on your values and desires, and let yourself get caught up in something predictable and painful? It's okay. Remember, you're a human being. We all make mistakes but also have an opportunity to learn from them.

Personal access to power, choice, and self-love is possible with a clean or a cleaner slate. You'll

- See clearly what's next for you.
- Forgive those around you.
- Feel lighter as more possibilities open up.
- Sigh, release, and relax your shoulders; and…
- Know that the love you crave is possible. Isn't that wonderful?

Got Forgiveness?

You may experience a sting of sadness and regret after completing this exercise. "How could I have let this happen?" you may ask yourself. You might beat yourself up after realizing the failure of many of your relationships was at your own hands. Forgive yourself and all your relationship mistakes. You did your best with what you knew about relationships at the time. Breathe through it. This is part of your discovery process. You're probably harder on yourself than those you may have harmed would be on you.

Forgiveness is a choice and journey. Notice if you have any blame, shame, or feelings of guilt specifically toward yourself. Lean into your thoughts, feelings, and body sensations. Notice what your body, mind, and heart are telling you. It's going to be okay. You were simply trying to love in the best way you knew how. It's in the past now. You're finally doing something about how you'll give and receive love in the present and the future. That's a beautiful thing, and I congratulate you for taking on this courageous work. Now, what will you do to celebrate yourself?

CHAPTER SIX

HEAL THY SELF HEALTHY SELF

> "The wound is the place where the light enters you."
> - Rumi

Sitting together in her car, I read my letter aloud. It was one of the most cathartic moments I've ever felt. I shared **my** experience of our relationship. I took complete responsibility for how (*a*) it went, (*b*) I interpreted it, and (*c*) I made up the story about what I did and didn't learn about our relationship.

We both sobbed, and my entire body shook as I shared what was on that page. I poured my heart and soul out to her. Tears hit the page as they blurred my vision. The pain inside me came to the surface. It was moving out of me as I began to start the long journey of healing. It was one of the ugliest cries I've ever had—raw, vulnerable, and painful. I leaned over, and she held me. "You finally get what it was like," she said.

"I do," I replied as my voice trembled.

This moment was the first time I truly related to her as a person. She was doing her best with an experience she never signed up for. It was my very first relationship—the relationship that I had with my mother as her son. My mother provided my first experience of what it meant to interact and be in a relationship. This was never a romantic relationship, and it pains me that I must qualify that fact. But it was my first relationship with another human being.

Her relationship with my father ended abruptly when he went to work one morning and never returned home. He was found unconscious in his truck, lifeless and pale. Paramedics worked on him for over an hour; what they brought back wasn't my father. Physiologically, it never could be. His brain went too long without oxygen, and he was brain-dead. When my mom withdrew life support a few days later, he held on for almost a month before passing on.

After my mother's relationship ended with my dad, she was a widow with two fatherless seven and eleven-year-old boys. With no instruction book to handle what came next, we limped along as a family as we figured out what new challenges would face us each day. We struggled and became survivors. We had no other choice. The only other alternative wasn't an option.

Reconciliation

I forgave my mom in the letter I wrote and shared it that night. Before that point, I held onto all my pain and blamed her. It was pain that unknowingly shaped and molded me throughout childhood, my formative years, and adulthood. I finally saw she did the best she could with the cards she was dealt. She did what she did, **and** she didn't do what she didn't do. I got what I received from her and didn't get what I didn't get. That was it. I was finally complete with my childhood.

We could finally be people with each other. The resentment, anger, fear, shame, blame, and guilt came to a place of understanding. It no longer needed to define who we were as a mother to her son, and as a son to his mother. These were simply the facts. Her husband died. My father died. Period.

How Did I Get Here?

I learned about therapy shortly after my father died. To help us process what happened and what was taking place next, my mother enrolled my brother and me in therapy to help us process what was happening. From what I remember, we both hated it. All we wanted was our father back. In addition to everything being turned upside down, we had to spend Wednesday evenings with a therapist. His name was John. I hated John immediately; he was a strange, funny-looking man to my seven-year-old eyes. I also don't remember much of the content of our conversations, but it was probably, "I want my dad back. I hate my brother. My mom is mean."

As a seven-year-old, that was all I could process. How could I have processed anything else? I remember dreaming about my father coming home. I dreamed about finding him in the woods during my many secret hikes into the forest preserve. I kept those wandering hikes a secret because I'd get in trouble if my mother knew I was alone in the forest. I would watch out my bedroom window, expecting and hoping he would come home. He never did. He couldn't.

Our family was wrought with drama, grief, and paralysis from the unknown. We barely survived on my mom's tips as a waitress. Some nights, I put ketchup on a slice of bread and called it pizza. My mother's grief was overwhelming, and I often remember waking up and hearing her cry in the middle of the night. She was crying over her lost love, dreams, and hopes for the future she wanted to give her children.

Mother grew up in an abusive household; the product of an illegitimate pregnancy. The bastardization of her life followed her until she left home at sixteen. She did the best she could with what she had. She's still one of the strongest, most determined women I know. She refused to fail; however, her childhood and the trauma of her dead husband left her with limited coping skills to compassionately raise two boys as a widow. We were in survival mode. Everyone was out for themselves.

Here Comes the Shit Storm

Many years later, the trauma of my childhood caught up to me. I distinctly remember a moment when I chose anger. I decided to rebel and be hurt, wanting the world to hurt as much as I did. I was clueless how to express what I was going through emotionally, so I expressed it physically. It started with cutting myself with razor blades. I punched things until my knuckles bled. I went to heavy-metal concerts and slammed my body as hard as possible into others. I did whatever I could to physically feel the pain I felt emotionally.

Trent Reznor of the band Nine Inch Nails has an incredible lyric from the song "Hurt," which sums up the entire internal landscape of what I felt. The lyric describes how he hurt himself just to see if he could still feel anything.

Causing physical pain was the only effective way I knew to heal emotionally. Guess what? It was a terrible idea. It didn't work; it was all I could do to process what was happening and physically feel the emotional pain. Self-destruction helped me express the rage and anger boiling inside. This led to more therapy, emergency interventions, tears, screaming, running away, fights, and even more holes in walls. Eventually, through a crippling addiction to prescription painkillers and a subsequent journey into sobriety and recovery, I learned new, healthier ways to process life and what was happening in my internal landscape. I discovered the critical importance of mental health from this experience, and I'm so grateful I did.

I've been in and out of therapy since age seven but didn't understand its importance until the apex of my addiction left me kneeling and begging for help. I'm active in my healing journey and work with an incredible team of healers. Therapists, energy healers, and specialized treatments all play an essential role in who I get to be as a man, husband, father, coach, leader, and human being.

Eventually, it became normal to talk about feelings and process what was happening within. When I stopped resisting the process and allowed myself to verbalize whatever and whenever, the benefits were clear. My mood, attitude, and outlook on life shifted, becoming more positive. Now I generally have access to high levels of joy, happiness, and fulfillment.

I get it. Some people don't like therapy or any healing process. That's true with some of my clients. Either they've never explored therapy, or they feel something must be wrong with utilizing a therapist. Therapy affirms it. You're forced to face the truth that you might be a little—or a lot—fucked up. It can also bring about the stigma you're somehow damaged goods. Here's **the truth:** who gives a shit?

If it could help, then why wouldn't you be willing to explore the possibilities? If taking on therapeutic work helped you show up as more authentic and joyful in your relationships, then wouldn't it be worth it? Are you open to see if it can do that for you?

We've **all** got emotional baggage. We may not be aware, but we **all** got baggage. No one grows out of childhood unscathed or unharmed. It's impossible. At some point, you learn that life and people can be harmful. A situation or someone left you feeling unsafe, so you were forced to put up your guard. It could be a moment as simple as being scolded for breaking something or as severe as being abused. Regardless of the event, you learned that terrible experiences could happen with the people you love or who should be loving you.

Coaching is Not Therapy. Coaching is Not Therapy.

As a relationship coach, I don't address therapeutic issues. These issues include anxiety, depression, obsessive compulsion, addiction, and others. Consider the issues requiring a proper mental health diagnosis by talking with a therapist, psychologist, or psychiatrist. Although it's common to experience these issues while coaching, diagnosing, or treating them isn't within my scope. I'm not trained or licensed to support clients in a therapeutic or counseling manner. However, as a coach, I'm responsible for speaking to clients in a caring, loving way if I sense there may be an opportunity for them to explore these things with qualified professionals if it could improve their mental health. I invite you to address them with a therapeutic professional. I've struggled with depression, addiction, and anxiety throughout my life regarding learning to love others and myself.

The conversations I engage in with clients are based on the present as we move toward the big, beautiful, seemingly-impossible future they want to create. I support my clients as they identify what they want and what's in the way. Then we create action plans and structures for accountability to achieve their goals. I also connect them to discover who they need to be and who they already are to create that future. Clients find a type of clarity, direction, power, and possibility that they didn't previously know or access.

Coaching can, and often does, open past issues as you expose the obstacles, or blocks, as we call them in coaching, standing in your way. Seemingly unknown to you for years, the process can spotlight parts of yourself previously covered and protected. Years of holding complaints from unmet needs and pushing feelings down can come to the surface. I give my clients permission to (*a*) dream what they want to dream, (*b*) be who they know themselves to be, and (*c*) become entirely responsible for what holds them back. That naturally brings up old pain, and if you're willing to explore those places, the process becomes one of the greatest gifts you can give yourself.

As a coach, I rarely address the past fully. In a future-based conversation, the past doesn't matter—nope! I get curious because there's much information to discover about how the past shaped you and how it impacts you today. From a coaching perspective, the past doesn't matter—until it does. When the past pulls and holds you back or repeatedly sabotages you, it's time to address it professionally.

I partner with several excellent therapists to ensure my clients are fully supported. Most of them are working with or have worked with a therapist. We have that conversation when and if it appears that the grip of the past harm and trauma refuses to let up. When more support is needed, we talk about a referral to a therapist. It's a tag-team approach. The past is addressed with a therapist, and the future is created with me as your coaching partner.

I believe one reason why you don't have the relationships you want is that the past is probably impacting you in the present and holding you back from your future. Is this impact worth exploring? I suggest that it is. Become willing to get the support you need to create what you want. Coaching combined with therapy is like rocket fuel to create the life and relationships of your dreams.

You Are Not Crazy

In my conversations, I've found a stigma still exists among some people who seek mental health treatment. Hell, even talking about our feelings is frowned upon. If this describes you, be open to anything that supports you. Remember, you're reading this book for a reason. You're looking for a different result. I invite you to be open to any action that supports you. Ask yourself, if working with a therapist moved you closer to finding the love of your life, then would you do it? If not, then why not? Do you judge yourself? Are you concerned about what others may think? Who cares? Think about what's possible, not what others or your critical, judgmental self may think.

Let's be clear. You're not broken. There's nothing wrong with you. There's no problem; there's only opportunity. Consider the parts of you that need healing. You've been wounded and need attention. Years of heartbreak, damaged relationships, devastating loneliness, and complex family and childhood dynamics have all shaped and created the framework in which you experience relationships. As I mentioned before, no one gets out of childhood unscathed. No one goes through multiple heartbreaks without getting a little fucked up. The wound is there. Trust me. It may be buried under layers of avoidance and distraction, but it's there.

Car Crash of Possibility

At the beginning of writing this book, a woman named Dawn hired me and inspired me to write this chapter. She achieved all the success anyone could want. She had a great career using her gifts to help others. She had a fantastic home that looked like it came out of a *Crate & Barrel* catalog. She took exquisite care of her body, mind, and soul. Dawn often engaged in yoga retreats, spiritual meditations, and travel to far-off destinations. She had it all—except she wanted a relationship leading to a forever commitment, children, partnership, and friendship. She tried creating that relationship for years to no avail. A chance encounter between us opened her up to the possibility of working with a coach for support.

During our first couple of sessions, I typically grew curious about the relationship patterns of a new client. I naturally questioned where she learned how to maintain relationships. There was a gaping chasm in Dawn's ability to open up, express herself, and be fully vulnerable. It occurred that she learned being vulnerable posed huge risks. So I asked her about any traumas in her relationships while growing up or early on in her dating experiences.

She paused. "There was the accident in high school," she hesitantly shared.

"Are you open to telling me a little more?" I invited her to share.

Dawn began to share a terrible experience when her first relationship ended horrifically. The boy she was romantically involved with tragically died in a car accident. She was a passenger in the car. She shared a lot more about what it was like to go through; but didn't feel it impacted her present relationships much. As our sessions continued, it was clear that this was a block from her past that affected her ability to move forward thirty years later.

I referred Dawn to a therapist for some short-term work. After a couple of sessions with a therapist, she shared how surprised she was about the amount of sorrow and emotion she still felt concerning this accident. She finally uncovered some of the fear and protection she firmly locked in place. Dawn guarded herself protectively in every relationship she'd ever entered. She held back her thoughts, feelings, and actions because she feared the relationship would end unexpectedly anyway. So why bother?

As an adult, she knew this wouldn't always be the case, but her fear was subconsciously at play. The memory impacted her ability to express herself fully in a relationship. Allowing herself to be all in with a partner was dangerous for Dawn. To open her heart so she felt exposed was too great a danger. As a result, Dawn limited her authenticity regarding how she showed up with her partners.

Ultimately, she and her partner were left feeling unfulfilled and wanting more. Dawn just completed our weekly session together at the time of this writing. She continues working with a therapist as well. As I gently push her forward into the future that she wants, therapy supports her by healing her past, helping her build courage, and teaching her faith that she can have what she wants. Therapy or coaching alone creates remarkable results, but when both disciplines are used together, the results are extraordinary. I speak from personal experience as well.

Because Dawn is now loving herself enough to take on her healing journey, she has opened the door to a whole new possibility in her experience of relationships. She knows exactly what she wants and who she is. She's connected to her gifts and her highest and best self. Dawn is living her purpose as she creates and manifests the love and relationship she wants. When I asked her about the most significant benefit she has received from working with me so far, she replied that it got her into therapy.

What did you get from my story and the story of Dawn? Do you have a wound tugging at you? Are you protecting part of yourself that would make you act differently once it became unprotected? Create the courage to address it since there may be devastating consequences if you don't. Next, you'll read the story of how I broke into someone's house for love. It's a doozie.

CHAPTER SEVEN
DON'T EVER LEAVE ME

> "Many of us live in denial of who we truly are because we fear losing someone or something—and there are times that if we don't rock the boat, too often the one we lose is ourselves..."
>
> - Dennis Merritt Jones

Soaking wet, surrounded by three pit bulls, I stood there trembling and shaking in a drug dealer's house. I was blind with rage, hurt, sad, and confused. My first wife was leaving me, and I went to the extreme to get her back.

I needed relief because she was sitting on the couch with another man, drinking a bottle of Pinot Noir and eating Brie. She started seeing someone while we separated, and I couldn't leave her alone or let her go. At this exact moment, I realized I'd gone too far—way too far. I knew something had to change and change immediately, or I'd hurt myself or someone else.

After a few weeks into our separation, we decided to trade in our more expensive vehicle for a less expensive one since she would be taking over the payments. There were signs all around that the marriage was ending, but I couldn't believe it. I was waiting for some magical memory to remind us of who we were when we fell in love and said, "I do" to each other. Now, too much hurt laid between us to reconcile what we once had. Our marriage was going to be over, and I had no idea how to get through it.

While we were at the car dealership going through the necessary and painful paperwork to sell and purchase a new vehicle, I read a text message on her phone without her permission. I was going crazy, filled with fear and regret. That's when I saw a text from another man; he was someone I knew and considered a friend. The message said, "Counting the hours until I get to see you." It was a romantic gesture and one familiar to me as we courted, but now it was coming from another man. It landed like a death blow.

Later that night, we went our separate ways, and I began going a bit insane. I started putting together all the pieces that pointed to their friendship becoming more. I reviewed phone records that showed hundreds of text messages to his number and hour-long phone calls. I began thinking about the conversations they had at parties, the looks they exchanged with each other, and how she looked whenever someone mentioned his name. It all came flooding in, and my thoughts began to drown me. In hindsight, I saw it all; that night, I knew in my soul that they were together.

I called and texted her, but she didn't respond. Pacing in my condo, I tried to talk myself out of finding them together, but I knew I must know; see them both in the act of betrayal. The obsession grew more intense as the night went on. I remember feeling so alone, scared, angry, and betrayed. The shame surrounding everything I had done to chase this incredible woman out of our marriage crippled me. I deserved all of it.

A few months earlier, I admitted myself into a treatment program for drugs and alcohol. I suffered from addiction and substance abuse for nearly a year. All my relationships suffered, and my marriage suffered the worst. I lost everything, and the one relationship I counted on most was slipping away. I was desperate and acted out of desperation. My physical body was healed, but my emotional and mental state had just begun its recovery journey. I don't know why my life took this course, but it provided the catalyst for everything I have today; As a newly sober graduate, I didn't have the faculty to navigate the overwhelming heartbreak coming my way like a tsunami.

The Event

It was 11:30 p.m. on an April evening in Chicago. Rain was pouring down and beginning to transition into sleet. April in Chicago is like the transition between winter and spring. A tug of war occurs between the change of the seasons, and winter was winning this night, so it was cold—freezing. I couldn't take any more of the obsessive thoughts, fear, and pain. I had to see it with my eyes to make our ending real.

I ran out of the condo and grabbed my old mountain bike. I jumped on it and began pedaling three miles to his house. In the dark of night, the wet avenues were glowing by the streetlights as they guided me on the path to devastation. Wearing a t-shirt and jeans, I felt the cold night bite at my arms and a face full of warm, rolling tears. I knew they'd be there. Intuition told me so.

Once at his street, I began surveying parked cars like a predator as I looked for the new car my soon-to-be ex-wife purchased just hours before my meltdown. Looking side to side, I saw the gold paint on the car. There it was. The color jumped out and stabbed me in the heart like a dagger. Our old license plate was lifelessly staring back on her new, gold Nissan Maxima. The plate mocked me with what we once had. All of it was gone now. I hated that damn car and what it represented even more: the end of a marriage.

"She's fucking here!" I thought. I tried not to believe it, but it was true. She was in his house. Frozen with fear and knowing what I was about to do, I surveyed the front of the house and the six-foot, wrought-iron gate, It was a blockade, and confirmation of my heartbreak, standing in front of me. I laid my bike on the sidewalk and quietly pulled myself up. Leaping off the top of the gate, I landed in the front yard, hearing a pop because I twisted my ankle. I limped to the front door and stopped. "What am I doing?" I asked myself during a brief pause.

In my insanity, I didn't want to give them a clue to my presence. They didn't deserve the luxury of getting themselves together to answer my questions and accusations. I was going to catch them red-handed in the act of infidelity and betrayal. I walked around the side of the house and checked the side door by turning the knob hard while pushing my full weight into the door. There was a creak and then a snap. The door was open. I was inside.

I went to the basement first. Then I looked around the maze of rooms that awaited. A shiver from the cold bicycle ride entered my bones as my heart clawed its way through my throat, awaiting the anticipation of what I'd find. I started seeing red and heard my heartbeat pulse in my eardrums. The sound was deafening. My muscles tightened, as my breath became increasingly rapid. I turned into a ferocious animal, backed into a corner, ready to attack and do whatever was required for survival.

The basement was damp and smelled old and musty. It was clear they weren't there. The silence against my heartbeat was deafening. I found steps leading to the first floor and began to climb. Each step upward fueled my rage and heartbreak. Unsure of what I might see once upstairs, I kept climbing steadily and quietly, so they weren't alerted to the intruder.

I reached the door, opened it slowly and looked to my right to see an empty kitchen. I heard tapping on the floor and felt a cold wetness on my left hand. One of his pit bulls walked over and sniffed the intruder who entered their home. I turned to the left—and there they were— sitting on the couch with an immediate look of shock and horror on their faces.

He jumped up and said, "Dude, what the fuck?" My wife sat there in early stages of surprise and utter devastation. She began sobbing. I was frozen. What the hell was I doing? What was the intention for coming down here? It was like being in a blackout. I felt sanity return, and I immediately became aware as if I was startled awake into a state of total and utter confusion.

She sobbed, "You're trying to make me into a bad person."

I said, "I'm not, but now I know it's over." She was legally still my wife, but our vows and bonds to each other were broken. I broke them years before.

It was the beginning of (*a*) the end, (*b*) my healing, and (*c*) my transformational work. This event became one of the most pivotal experiences of my journey—one for which I'm equally horrified and grateful. I could've easily been shot, attacked by dogs, or beaten up. I could have physically hurt them or myself. Thankfully, none of that happened.

I walked toward the front door with my head hung low. What was I thinking? I was driven by fear, sadness, anger, and frustration, like a wild animal backed into a corner and ready to lash out at anyone who came close. My wounds were real, and I had no one to blame but myself for how I reacted. Thank God for a moment of sanity that returned. I believe it kept us all safe from what I could have done.

I opened the front door and walked down the steps. The cold rain bit my face. A wave of relief enveloped me. The marriage was over. I walked through the gate and grabbed my bicycle. Then I headed back to my empty house—a place that was no longer home but the holding cell of my failed marriage. The next day I moved to my parent's house.

Codependency

I am not an expert on attachment or codependency. There are individuals far more intelligent and more versed in therapeutic recovery from codependency. I am, however, an expert in what it means to be codependent. The story above demonstrates it. My wife, in such a codependent state, had an obligation to (*a*) be my caretaker, (*b*) manage my feelings, and (*c*) comfort me. Without her, I was lost. It wasn't until I broke into the house I realized there was a problem. If not addressed, it would surely repeat itself in my next relationship. The clarity that came that moment was one of the greatest gifts I've ever received. Here's the message I got—**no one has the power to change your life except you.**

I was hoping, wishing, and demanding that my soon-to-be ex would make me feel better, fix me, and make me whole. I relied upon her and others to give what I needed. I took no responsibility for being the one to love, care for, and comfort myself. I also had no idea what I was doing. It was deeply embedded in (*a*) who I was as a man, (*b*) my needs, real or imagined, and (*c*) my ability to give and receive love. There was a void no one could fill but me, although unconsciously I demanded others do so. I was sick, and the only cure for the illness was to take complete responsibility for my happiness and relationships.

During that moment, while standing there trembling in his living room, I felt a powerful sense of release. A wave of comfort washed over me. I almost passed out on the floor in a heaping pile of skin and bones. I knew at that moment that only I had the power to change my life and relationships. It was up to me—no one else. The weight of the world was lifted, and a sensation started to light up and grow. It was **hope.**

In addition to the relief I felt, I also felt a surge of power, almost like a spiritual experience. Right then and there, I understood the inner work I needed to do and how necessary it was for me to embark upon. To ever have a chance at love and a meaningful relationship, I had to change—and change I did.

The Aftermath

I was truly sick concerning my approach to relationships. I was an insatiable, rapacious monster doing whatever it took to feel loved. I didn't love myself, and it became the sole responsibility of my partners to bear that burden. Eventually, they would become exhausted and would leave. It all finally made sense. I would have left too.

My divorce stung the most because I thought we'd be together forever. She would never leave because of our vows and our agreement to have and hold each other in sickness and health. But the marriage was a prison for her and a cage for me. The divorce was one of the greatest gifts I've ever received. Over time, we worked through a lot with each other during our separation and eventual divorce. We became friends and came to a place where we could share what was going on with us without the need to make it mean anything about each other. I continued with my recovery. She, too, has gone on to marry again and is happier than ever in her relationship journey.

What's In It for You?

Although you're reading this book to learn differences between healthy and unhealthy relationships, simply having relationship issues in your past is not a diagnosis of codependency. A saying we have in coaching is that it's just "a place to look." Explore it to see if there is any value for you.

If you have codependent tendencies, practice noticing them. They may be subtle or painfully outright and in your face. Regardless, I invite you to be honest. Be honest with what you expect from your partner. They are not with you to fix you. They don't owe you anything. They are with you to share a journey of love and relationship with you—together in partnership—making each of you experience the whole sum of life better.

I'll share some resources to support your understanding of codependency toward the end of this chapter. Here are a few traits of codependency you or your partner may have:

◆ Low self-esteem
◆ People pleasing
◆ Caretaking
◆ Reactive

- ◆ Manipulative
- ◆ Controlling
- ◆ Poor boundaries
- ◆ Denial
- ◆ Obsessive
- ◆ Lack of intimacy
- ◆ Painful emotions

The first step in understanding if codependency negatively impacts your relationships is to generate awareness about how you are in a relationship. The traits on this list aren't intended to make you or your partner wrong. It is, however, an opportunity to improve your experience of relationships. Codependency can be insidious and disastrous, causing conflict or making it a million times worse. Explore where you are, where your partner is, and what would serve both of you best.

When Jane and I began working together, I was curious about how little we talked about her. Any question I asked her ended up being answered as a complaint about her partner, Carl. It was like she couldn't hear. As a coach, sometimes it's appropriate to sit back and let a client vent, but this was more than venting. Jane accused Carl of everything and pretended she had no part in it.

"What can you be responsible for?" I asked.

He just doesn't….." Jane began to answer.

"I'm going to interrupt you," I said. "Do you notice that you don't answer my questions? It all comes back to blaming Carl. Willing to take a look here? What can you be responsible for?" I asked again.

Jane was willing, and this began an honest look at who she was in her relationship. She was unable to even consider that she was half responsible for the relationship. Instead of becoming curious about the dynamics playing out and connecting with her partner, she accused and blamed him for how he didn't adequately meeting her needs.

We wholeheartedly explored her needs. I challenged them at times, and she noticed how Carl would never be able to meet her needs in their current relationship. It was nearly impossible. We started small by getting her to voice her needs. Then we explored how she could meet those needs herself. After, we explicitly began talking about her codependent tendencies with Carl. This opened the relationship up for exploration, understanding, and partnership. Jane and Carl are **together** for the first time in their relationship. They are not in a proving match or fixing situation. They are learning what it means to love each other and each be responsible while doing so.

Resources

There are several resources available to those experiencing codependency. If anything in this chapter resonates with you, I encourage you to explore the following resources to support your relationship journey and possible recovery. Becoming responsible for who are you is one of the most powerful, loving things you can do for yourself and your partner. Be honest, open to exploring the message, and willing to receive it.

Books:

Codependent No More: How to Stop Controlling Others and Start Caring for Yourself by Melody Beattie. This is like the Bible of codependency.

You're Not Crazy – You're Codependent by Jeanette Elisabeth Menter.

Controlling People: How to Recognize, Understand, and Deal with People Who Try to Control You by Patricia Evans.

Support Groups:

Codependents Anonymous (CoDA) is a 12-step support group.
https://www.coda.org

Alcoholics Anonymous (AA) is a 12-step support group.
https://www.aa.org

Adult Children of Alcoholics (ACA) & Dysfunctional Families is a 12-step support group.
https://www.adultchildren.org

Narcotics Anonymous (NA) is a 12-step support group.
https://www.na.org

CHAPTER EIGHT
ALL HOPE IS GONE

"Hope is a waking dream."
- Aristotle

How many times have you wanted to give up? Suppose you look over the course of your relationships. I bet you'll find some examples: another terrible date, another serious conversation with your partner resulting in no change, or even worse, the collection of evidence that you're indeed unlovable. Something must be wrong with you or wrong with them. There must be, right? There seems to be no other explanation. You see others getting what you want. They're going out on great dates, meeting incredible people, and from the looks of it, having a fantastic time finding love. What are you doing wrong?

I had a client who hired me to help her find a relationship. She had it all except the man she wanted. Carol was sweet. She was soft-spoken, tender, and a bit timid. There seemed to be a scared little girl inside her that was running the show and holding her back. When I took Carol as a client, I shared what it would be like to work with me; she would need to commit to four months at a minimum and most likely six to nine months if she was going to achieve the goal she wanted. It takes months to uncover how, why, and where we get stuck.

Carol worked with me for two months and then vanished. I had no idea where she went. She missed our calls and stopped paying for her contracted time. Carol didn't respond to my calls, emails, or texts. She ghosted me. I never take this sort of thing personally. I can't. This was Carol's stuff, not mine. Coaching can bring up many old painful patterns and trauma. So people who feel confronted by these experiences will sometimes bail. She also hired me to break her shit up so she could get a different result. Since this seemed like a typical behavior Carol engaged in throughout her relationships, I became curious.

She finally responded to one question: "Is this how it normally goes for you in your relationships—you disappear?" Carol called back almost immediately. She was doing what she knew how to do when she didn't feel like she was getting what she wanted. This time she was doing it to me, her coach, but I wouldn't play that game, so I called her on it.

She owned up to her game-playing and said thank you. We were two months into our work together, and people typically want to quit when triggered by their old pain, patterns, and trauma. She shared the fact that she tends to feel the same after two months in a relationship. If she senses her needs aren't met, she ghosts or disappears.

I emphasized to Carol she never gave me a chance to make a difference for her with coaching. If she wasn't getting her needs met in our coaching relationship, it was up to her to communicate. After years of failed relationships, the lack of fulfillment she repeatedly experienced from our coaching sessions led her to believe that her needs didn't matter. So why bother bringing them to our sessions? We created a plan of action for Carol to express her needs in all aspects of her life; in her romantic, platonic, familial, and professional relationships to ensure her well-being. Not only was it great practice for Carol, but it was also constant self-reflection. It is not my job to meet my client's needs, but I'm here to support them in getting their needs met from within and by others in their life. I'm a mirror for their gaps in action. In doing so, I empower them to bridge those gaps.

I admit that finding and creating the relationship you want can be exhausting if you relate to it that way. You have to choose to connect to it that way. I suggest you consider the following perspective: the process itself isn't exhausting, but how you internalize the process to provide clues about your identity is exhausting.

For example, you may think, "I was ghosted again—that must mean I'm not attractive enough."

What do you want? How do you know? You made that up. Is it true? Is it a fact that would hold up in a court of law or simply an interpretation of a situation you turned into a narrative about yourself? Your experience doesn't necessarily mean anything about you. It's an excellent opportunity to become more well-informed, but it doesn't have to be about you.

Resignation Kills

When it comes to getting what you want, resignation will kill any chance of receiving it. Resignation works; in the end, you never get what you want because you give up and quit. Giving up on what you want is one of the easiest things to do when it comes to achieving your goals. Think of all the times that you were motivated to accomplish a goal. A quick scan of your memory should land you somewhere close to (*a*) a New Year's resolution, (*b*) a dream from childhood, (*c*) taking that trip, (*d*) getting that degree, (*e*) becoming famous, (*f*) writing that book, or (*g*) whatever. You were motivated. You got distracted. You became unmotivated. You quit.

Motivation is bullshit. Motivation won't pull you through the darkness to the other side. Motivation allows you to give up when it's no longer there. There must be something higher and more powerful than motivation to keep you going. Motivation is a feeling, and feelings don't last. You haven't been happy forever. You haven't been sad forever. You certainly won't be motivated forever.

As humans, we're built to give up. It's sad but true. We're built to create and sustain maximum levels of comfort to survive. We recoil from discomfort. When you give up, you're merely surviving. There is a threat so you're pushing away. You're retreating from discomfort. Unfortunately, you're also withdrawing from what you want most: love, relationship, partnership, passion, intimacy, joy, or celebration. So when the discomfort of this process gets too painful, humans resign. Do any of the following statements sound familiar?

- "I'll probably die alone."
- "I'll be the crazy cat lady."
- "I'm going to switch teams."

- "Who needs 'em anyway?"
- "You would give up, too, if they did this to you."
- "No one wants me anyway."

Resignation is a dangerous game if you're truly invested in creating your ideal relationship. It gives you an out and lets you quit. It makes the goal the problem. You get to blame the person, the circumstance, or the story you've made about yourself. Ultimately, you give up and don't have to become responsible for your wants. Resignation is a cop-out.

Be courageous and demand the love that you want. Keep going in the face of a million reasons to quit. After all, you're only quitting on yourself. You deserve all the love and affection that you seek.

Attachment Thrills

When it comes to getting what you want, attachments will kill any chance of receiving it. Attachment works every time; in the end, you never get what you want. Like resignation, being attached to your expectations of how relationships should be is every bit as dangerous as giving in to resignation. It feels good to be right about how this all **must occur**. But you're insisting on being right about being wrong. Sorry—not sorry. Attachment severely limits what's possible for you in creating the relationship you want.

It creates false hope that you'll get what you want **only** when all these factors fall perfectly and precisely into place. Attachment holds onto what you want and how you get it. You become attached to the how, when, and where you'll meet your person. You become attached to who you think they are, what it will be like being with them, and who you get to be when you're with them.

Then what happens? You set yourself up for disappointment. If the show doesn't go as planned, you become sad, frustrated, and (yep) resigned. Being attached to how a relationship is supposed to be won't serve you. Be open—completely open—to any experience or person that comes your way. Now, that doesn't mean lowering your standards, but notice that if you're so attached, it limits your possible partners or experiences.

We can create attachments to such unrealistic expectations from fear and scarcity that we essentially build a wall around our hearts. It's a covert way to protect our hearts from future heartbreak. I never suggest that you lower your standards. In fact, I coach my clients to double down on their standards. Notice if what you have in place is created to either protect or simply guide you as it should be. Whether you're resigned or overly attached, neither will serve you to find love.

It's a Choice

You must choose to give up. It may not feel like it, but the moment you become resigned is the moment you decide to give up. You can look at all the ways and evidence you want about why it makes sense, practically speaking. Yet it's all reduced to a straightforward question: Does resignation and giving up push you closer to what you want, or does it pull you further away? I assume you can see it pulls you further away. Can we agree on this? Good.

If you've resigned and are still in the game, this won't be fun. Going into a date expecting the worst, blowing off a date, or ghosting people on dating apps will catch up with you. Not taking exquisite care of yourself will catch up with you too. I firmly believe you'll attract what you put out there. If you believe a date will suck—then guess what—it will indeed suck. If you blow off dating and match inquiries, you'll be blown off too. If you stop taking care of yourself, you'll attract the same behavior in others. Be what you want to attract. How you react internally and externally will have consequences in your process.

Everything you choose has a consequence. There's a consequence to giving up. The likelihood of finding and creating what you want narrows considerably when you mentally and emotionally resign yourself and give up. Choosing to continue and sticking with it will put you face-to-face with some potentially uncomfortable situations. So can you be uncomfortable in service to what you want? Is it worth it? If you had to go on one more awful date or get ghosted one more time, would you be willing to do it if there was a possibility of finding your ideal relationship on the other side?

If you have a bad experience, will you let it (*a*) define you, (*b*) impact your next action, or (*c*) take you out of the game entirely? Or will you receive it for what it is, merely information? Will you stay firm in your resolve to create the love and relationship you want? You always have a choice—always. What will you choose?

Hey, I get it. It gets tough, and if you look for it, you can find all the reasons why you're right about how bad it is out there; but you'll only succeed when you choose to be better and overcome those reasons. You may be saying, "Okay, I want to be better. But how?"

First, you must have hope. Second, you must fully commit to finding the love that you want. Finally, love yourself enough to make the difference you want for yourself. If you're not willing to overcome the disappointment and discomfort, you might as well stop reading this book. Put it down and return when your head and heart are open and willing to do what it takes. It's okay. The book will be available when you're ready.

Here's the How

If you're still reading, good for you. You're willing to move forward in the face of the unknown. Resignation hasn't left its mark, and you're moving above the fray. Take a moment and acknowledge yourself for that decision. You're venturing into the unknown. Like an explorer walking into uncharted wilderness, you're embarking on a new adventure.

Take a moment to connect with this moment. Consider where you've been, where you are, and where you want to go. When you think about how your relationships have occurred up until this point, acceptance will be one of the greatest gifts you can give yourself. Accept what has happened and accept what has not happened—period. The goal is to let it be what it is. If you're single, then you're single. If you're in a relationship that's not truly what you want, then let it simply be that. If you fear the future and what's to come, then accept that you're scared and skeptical of how things may go from here.

Acceptance is the answer. Acceptance is the answer. Acceptance is the answer.

Keep repeating these words until you believe them, and they become part of you. Acceptance is the answer. Accepting it all wherever you are will give you one of the greatest gifts you can give yourself: freedom. You'll no longer be held back by the past or present, so you're free to move forward. You can set out into your wilderness and explore what's to come.

In my journey to creating the relationship of my dreams, learning to accept how my previous relationships occurred up until the point I met my wife was critical. Before then, I blamed everyone and everything for how they happened. That wasn't fair to them, the Universe, or me. It stripped me of my power to do anything about it and left me as a victim. This was all happening **to me**, and I was left powerless and pissed off.

However, I knew I could have it happen differently. I had to **choose** for it to happen differently. It was up to me to take 100 percent responsibility for the experience I wanted and understand how it happened. My anger was about the past.

So who gives a shit? Why was I letting something that happened to me affect what could be happening now? It started to make zero sense that I let the past inform my future. I had to accept and let it go—all of it. So I did.

Day by day, I woke up and chose my past and future. My past was what it was, and my future was for me to create. It's not what I had to do but who I had to become to move forward. I had to learn to accept, trust and create the hope that what I wanted and who I wanted was out there. She was, and I had to get out of my way to let her in. I had to find out what worked for me to have that hope. Even today, I reinvent my hope daily. Whether it's in my relationships, business, health, or marriage, each day, I wake up and get to reinvent who I want to be.

Don't Give Up

The same will be valid for you. You get to choose and create what works for you. You may feel discouraged because the answer hasn't been given yet. That's because I don't know your answers. You do. I understand you want the *10 Steps to Acceptance and Letting Go,* but you won't get it from me.

If we were to work together, I'd help you pull your answers out for yourself. I trust my clients are the experts of their own lives once they get the limiting crap out of the way and become responsible. I call bullshit anytime I see a list of steps or keys, or secrets from a so-called self-development guru. How can anyone know what you truly need besides you? So that's your work from here on out: engage in your self-discovery.

Discover your road to acceptance. Accepting how your journey has occurred and how it's happening will allow room for your discovery. The resignation will dissipate, then you'll note the attachment and be filled with faith and trust. What you **genuinely want** is available to you. Unfortunately, as cliché as it is, what they say is true. Here are some of those typical cliches:

- ◆ Do your work.
- ◆ Live your life for you.
- ◆ Fall in love with yourself.
- ◆ Love yourself first before you love another.

CHAPTER NINE

MYTHS ABOUT RELATIONSHIPS

"If it's not making you better, it isn't love. True love makes you more of who you are, not less."

- Mandy Hale

Remember when you were taught about positive relationships during your formative years? The outline included (*a*) the specifics of what a successful relationship looks like, (*b*) the characteristics and qualities of a good partner, and (*c*) how those relationships should make you feel. Remember when you were taught the specifics of (*a*) what to say, (*b*) what to do, and (*c*) who to be to have the most successful relationships possible? Oh, you don't remember Relationships 101? Dang! Me neither! That type of education has never existed, but it should!

Somewhere along the way, you created beliefs about relationships and how they should be. Modeled effectively or perhaps tragically, you looked to your parents, other family members, friends, movies, books, and fantasies to create your paradigm of information about love and relationships. Somewhere along the way, the version of your ideal relationship wasn't taught but created by what you observed. Think about it. Can you recall when this was true in your childhood and young-adult life?

As a small child, I remember the cartoons I watched that gave me clues about the roles we play in relationships; the infatuated wolf chasing the sexy-looking chicken—a sexy chicken?—come on! Let's not forget the familiar movie where the strong man comforts an overly emotional woman or where a stern, cold woman punishes the children because her man/husband is away cheating with another woman—or another man. Relationships are complex and as unique as each individual in them. There is no accurate barometer for success. You likely picked up some myths about love and relationships on your journey. Spending a little time to review these myths is worthwhile. They may have started in some truth to explain your specific situation, but they damage how you authentically show up and relate to others in your relationships.

In the highly personal work I do with clients, we first uncover the story they tell themselves. The story is usually based on myths. The myth caused them to judge themselves critically and condemn their process of creating relationships. Chances are, it's a fabricated truth they carry with them to serve as facts regarding love and relationships. The remainder of this chapter will uncover the six most common relationship myths I encounter. Use this list as guidance and discover how to create a new, inspiring story about yourself and your relationship process.

Myth Number One: It Shouldn't be This Hard

Who says your relationship process will be hard when you think about it? If you're unclear, get up from where you're sitting and bring this book. Walk into your bathroom and look in the mirror. That's the person who's making it hard. Does that person look familiar? That person is you. Yes, I'm being a smartass, but I want to be sure you get the point. It's hard because you're choosing to view creating a relationship as complicated, difficult, and exasperating. "It shouldn't be this hard" is a myth because you control entirely how to relate to the relationship-building process.

You get to choose whether or not it's hard to create a relationship. Are you looking for all the reasons and evidence why it is hard? If you look, you'll find them. The reason you're probably reading this book is to overcome those same reasons. If you want your relationships to suck, you'll find evidence and explanations supporting your belief that creating a relationship is challenging. Or for everyone else to see how wronged, you've been. Congratulations! You got it! Does that serve you? Does that belief make you excited and invigorated about finding the love and relationship you want? My guess is it doesn't, and you must choose to let that shit go. It will be uncomfortable, but agree to let go of the belief about how hard it is to find love. Let go of it now because it's one of the most loving practices you can do for yourself.

If you agree to let go of the belief about how hard it is to find love and create relationships, then there's a place to begin creating one. You'll have enough energy to do the hard work of enduring the process of creating new relationships that don't end up like your old ones. Yep, I said it. I've asked you to let go of your perception about the difficulty of this process, but the process of letting go, in and of itself, can be arduous. To experience your relationships differently, this process will require the breakdown of your ego, forgiveness, the opening of your heart, and uncomfortable levels of vulnerability.

Can you perceive the work required for this journey as something other than arduous? How about perceiving it as an adventure? Choose to see it as an exploration to get what you **truly want**: to be loved the way you want and to create the ease and joy you want in life, love, and relationships. Do you believe a relationship is possible for you? It is, and it'll take work. So choose to relate to the relationship process as a gift.

Myth Number Two: It Will Work Out if it is Meant to Be

This is a dangerous myth because it assumes that neither of you should be responsible for creating the experience of your past, present, and future relationships. All relationships require attention, commitment, and work. Whether you're single and looking for your partner or part of a couple navigating their relationship, creating an ideal relationship must be intentional.

This myth is similar to jumping in your car, pushing the pedal to the floor, and then taking your hands off the steering wheel, hoping for the best. Good relationships take a lot of intentional work. Every day they invite you to (a) be yourself, (b) address your partner's needs as well as your own, and (c) be responsible for the type of love you want to experience. A relationship shouldn't happen to you. You should happen to your relationship.

My wife and I constantly get comments from people about how enamored we are of each other. When we're out eating dinner, we're often asked if it's our anniversary or if we're on our honeymoon. People are drawn to our love. It's a love we create and work at daily. We bring intention and complete responsibility for who we are in our marriage. We ask for what we need and share own fears and resentments. Shona and I also agree to continue improving for ourselves and each other daily. We created this type of love with each other and love it when others notice the fruits of our labor. When people share how they love our love, my favorite response is, "We work our asses off at it."

Myth Number Three: If You Really Loved Me, Then You Would Know What I Need

One evening while on a working vacation, my wife and I went for dinner. We were eating on a patio in beautiful Savannah, Georgia, after speaking to a few hundred entrepreneurs about the importance of cultivating personal and romantic relationships. We had a blast.

Now it was time to relax, celebrate, and enjoy the scenery. For me, it was time to ease down from being tightly wound. It was warm and sunny, although a bit humid for my liking, a wonderful, early-summer evening. I was thoroughly enjoying my meal, eating, relaxing—breathing in, breathing out—and just in love with it all.

I looked at my wife, and she was crying. I was concerned and confused at the same time. What did I miss? Did I say something, look at her wrong, or get caught unintentionally looking at another woman? Was I in trouble? What was going on with her?

"What's going on, love?" I asked. "Are we that boring old couple that doesn't talk anymore?" she sobbed. "What do you mean?" I replied. "We're not talking. We're just sitting here in silence," she shared. "Oh, babe, I'm just enjoying my dinner and your company," I said. "Oh, my God!" she laughed.

My wife felt lonely at that moment. She had an unmet need that she hadn't shared with me. I was oblivious to it. No one was wrong. She felt lonely and needed conversation and connection with me while I was content as hell and enjoying everything exactly as it was. In that beautiful moment, we reaffirmed the importance of voicing our needs to each other.

Over time we've learned to anticipate each other's needs. We can also ask for what we need or even ask the other if there is a need. Sometimes our needs are unknown, so we sit with each other and share affection.

Never assume your partner will know and understand your needs. You may also need to discover what your needs are by doing a little self-probing. Answer the following questions:

◆ What do you need from your relationship?
◆ What do you need when you feel sad or lonely?
◆ Who do you need to be for yourself when times feel tough?

Create this dialogue by frequently asking yourself what you need now, in the next moment, and so on. When you know your needs, you can communicate them. When your needs go unaddressed, you can become needy and act and choose your needs from an impoverished place. Practice getting your needs met from a responsible place.

Myth Number Four: If My Partner Would Just Change, Then…

Have you pointed a finger more toward others than at yourself? Many of us are experts at the blame game regarding relationships. "If he would just do that." "If she would just do this." "I can't believe they blah blah blah." It's easier to shove the responsibility off to another person about how your relationship or quest to be in one is going. There is a high cost to that choice. It completely strips away your power. The ability to make the change you want to see in your partner starts with making that change in yourself.

If you truly want change, then be the change. Consider becoming a better partner. Be a better version of yourself for yourself. What can you practice to make the difference you want in your relationship? Can you be more open, forgiving, honest, willing, or expressive? What are you craving that you can create for yourself? Discover and explore the possibilities. Look at what you can do first. Then share your needs and co-create the relationship with your partner. One flame can light a million others.

Myth Number Five: Commitment Is a One-time Event

Commitment is a declarative act. You have declared your agreement to something with someone. Whether it's the agreement to (*a*) be mutually exclusive, (*b*) have an open relationship, or (*c*) get married, an agreement between you and another person is made. With this commitment, a container was formed for you to create what you want inside it. Many people get tripped up and begin taking things for granted. Well, we committed to each other, so that's done and over with.

Don't confine commitment to a single event like a wedding ceremony, dinner where both of you delete your dating apps, or the conversation you two had while sitting in the driveway. Treat commitment as a choice to be reinvented every single day. Don't take for granted what you have or will create. Start each day committing to who you'll be in the relationship with yourself. How do you want to show up to life each day? How do you want to show up for yourself? If you're in a relationship, how do you want to show up to your person? Perhaps declare who you'll be, then reflect throughout the day on your progress to determine if any adjustments or acknowledgments are needed. Next, commit to your current or future partner. Who will you be for them? What will you do? How will you act? If you already have a partner, bring them into our conversation and co-create your intentional declarations with them.

Myth Number Six: Getting Help Means There's a Problem

I'll admit, this one drives me absolutely nuts. Whether it's coaching or therapy, getting help means you're committed to creating something different for yourself. It's likely a better, more fulfilling experience than what you have. There should be no shame in getting support. Not getting any or enough support probably created what's happening for you now. Perhaps reading this book is more about trying to find solutions on your own. You're still on your own...but now with a book.

In my coaching practice and the couples practice I share with my wife, we often hear, "I would love to work with you, but we don't have any problems." I would like to present an analogy by asking the following question: When elite athletes hire coaches to get them to the Olympics, is it because there's a problem? Most likely not.

It's because they want to get to the next level of performance in their sport and achieve greatness. They want to see how far they can take their minds, bodies, and spirits. The same rationale applies to relationship coaching. My hat is off to you if everything is perfect and you're experiencing what you want. Celebrate your love! Woo-hoo!

If you're single, confused, and resigned when it comes to creating a relationship, then working with a coach would support you. If you want your experience to be different, do something you've never done. Getting help doesn't confirm that there's an issue. Instead, it demonstrates that you're committed to creating a different type of relationship. If you want deeper levels of intimacy, including more joy, freedom, ease, and spontaneity, then a coach will support you. Why wait until there's a problem to get support in your relationship?

So Now What?

To summarize, the following myths prevent you from creating the love that you want because it absolves you from taking your fair share of responsibility:

1. It shouldn't be this hard.
2. It will work out if it's meant to be.
3. If you loved me, you would know what I need.
4. If my partner would just change, then…
5. Commitment is an event.
6. Getting help means that there's a problem.

Although I've shared six of the most common myths I come across with my clients, this shouldn't be construed as the entire list of myths. It's a start. Review the list. Do any of the myths hit home a little too much? Is there one you feel doesn't apply to you or your relationships? Did I miss one or two? Spend a moment considering the myths you've created to explain the disappearing possibility of a fantastic relationship.

Have you created a myth to ease your broken heart? What other stories have you created to protect yourself? Do you notice a pattern in these myths? What else can you write down and explore?

Before meeting my wife, I spent much time discovering the stories and myths I told myself. This was an uncomfortable process and one I spent a couple of months uncovering. In compiling all the evidence of my failed relationships with women and with family, friends, and business colleagues—hell—I went back to high school. I learned one fundamental, prevailing belief I held. I believed I was unlovable.

It breaks my heart to write this and think about it now. I was so hard on myself. I always blamed myself for how relationships turned out; however, it wasn't just me. There was another person in those relationships with their own stories, myths, needs, and history. I didn't have to take all the fault.

Don't get me wrong, I'm happy most of those relationships ended as they did, but I question others. The point I want to hit home is the stories I told myself weren't factual. The prevailing story I was unlovable was an interpretation I made about myself. That's it. The truth is I deserve love. I had to believe in my lovability and create it within myself before expecting anyone else to love me as I wanted and needed to be loved. Just as I had my **unlovable story**, look for your prevailing story. Bust the myth you have about yourself and yourself in relationships. It no longer serves you.

"You, yourself, as much as anybody in the entire universe, deserve your love and affection."
- Sharon Salzberg

CHAPTER TEN

COMFORT ZONES

> "I've never seen any life transformation that didn't begin with the person in question finally getting tired of their own bullshit."
>
> - Elizabeth Gilbert

"Are you fucking kidding me? You want me to do what?" Maria wasn't having any of this as she yelled back over the phone. "I'm not doing that!" Maria's buttons were pushed, and she was letting me know in no uncertain terms.

Did I go too far by suggesting she do the unthinkable? To describe Maria in a word: power. She held herself like royalty—majestic. She was a petite woman with sharp facial features and a hilarious sense of humor. When she walked into a room, her tiny stature filled it up.

What elicited this response from Maria was my invitation for her to step into the unknown. I invited her to do something outside her comfort zone, and she was instantly terrified, and rightfully so. Anything outside our comfort zone is uncomfortable by definition. Maria was in a failing relationship and wanted support with her exit strategy. A couple of months went by with her declaring each week that she would bring the conversation up with her partner but week after week, during our calls, she reported that she made no progress. Unable to speak her truth to her partner, she remained in a relationship that no longer served her. Joy, happiness, and life were draining away from this powerful woman. She was becoming smaller and smaller the longer she stayed with him.

As a coach, I stand boldly in the face of the fear my clients experience. So I asked the bold question Dave asked me years before. "Maria, is it over with you and John?"

"Yes, I know it is," she replied.

"Great," I said, "Can you reach him on the phone right now?"

Hesitating, she said, "Yes, why?"

"Well, would you be willing to call and tell him right now? I'll wait on the other line."

The **bold thing** is a life-altering conversation. Once it's said, there's an understanding that there's no going back to what once was. Your life will change. Maria could have said no and pushed it off another day, week, or month, but she knew she had to do it.

Refer back to the first sentence of this chapter. Maria was confronted with doing the unthinkable. She had to face the scary, holy-shit-my-life-is-going-to-change-and-I-don't-like-how-this-feels moment. She called her partner to have **the talk** during dinner that night. She did it. She did the unthinkable, scary, holy-shit-my-life-is-going-to-change-and-I-don't-like-how-this-feels action. Maria knew what she wanted for months and probably even longer. More accurately, she knew what she didn't like in her relationship. When she got back on the phone, with a slight tremble in her voice, she said, "Thanks, Bob."

Highway to the Comfort Zone

What kept Maria in an unfulfilling relationship knowing she wanted to be out of it? It was her comfort zone. We all have comfort zones, a normal part of being human. A comfort zone is a psychological state where all things being experienced are known, predictable, comfortable, and non-threatening. Think of it like your warm, comfortable bed. You know, the bed with the mattress that has just the right amount of firmness (not too hard or soft); then think of your favorite pillow and the weight of the comforter—there's plenty of room to stretch as you feel the touch of your 1500-thread-count, Egyptian-cotton sheets. With this level of comfort, there's no reason to leave your bed. There's no danger; it's safe.

Imagine you're required to get out of your cozy, comfy bed because of a knock at the door, a ringing phone, a full bladder, a grumbling stomach, or a needy pet. To take care of whatever it is, you must get out of bed and leave your comfort zone to tackle the task at hand. Be willing to get uncomfortable to get what you want. The same requirement is necessary to create your big, scary relationship dreams. Since it may require levels of discomfort that you're unwilling to do to move toward, this is where accountability and support are critical. This accountability is precisely why Maria hired me, although she may not have known it at the time. She hired me to help her say those uncomfortable words.

Why would you purposely step outside your comfort zone? It's simple. What you **really want** is there. The fairytale relationship, the fulfilling love, the partnership, the until-death-do-you-part commitment, the toe-curling orgasms, the forever home, the Sunday snuggles, the vacations, the joy, the laughter, and the love on the other side of your discomfort. That's why.

Run through the fear and discomfort and right into the relationship of your dreams. I assert that everything you say you want and don't already have is outside your comfort zone. You must get uncomfortable to create it.

Read this. **Everything you say you want and don't already have is outside your comfort zone. You must get uncomfortable to create it.**

Print this and post it. Recite it over and over until you understand your discomfort is beautiful. It lets you know you're onto a bigger, better, unknown, and new relationship.

You Want Me to Do What?

We naturally dislike anything outside our comfort zone. Think of all the ways you avoid uncomfortable situations: public speaking, passing up that slice of pizza, hiring a personal trainer to get your butt in the gym, spending money on self-development, asking for what you need, jumping out of a plane, etc. The list could go on. So be more concerned with what's on the other side of your discomfort rather than focusing on avoiding it and returning to those familiar cozy, comfy feelings.

That public speaking gig could land you more clients, friends, and colleagues, opening you up to more opportunity and wealth. Passing up that pizza (one of the most uncomfortable actions I choose to do—ha!) and hiring a personal trainer makes you (1) feel better (more joyful), (2) look super sexy, and (3) be confident in bed. It also gives you access to the half of your closet full of the someday-I'll-fit-into-these skinny jeans/clothes. Spending money to get the support you need to live your best life can lead to crazy levels of fulfillment and joy. A happier you will attract more abundance in life everywhere. Asking for what you need gets your needs met. Crazy—I know—but it works. Imagine jumping out of a plane and experiencing the most exciting, terrifying, mind-blowing, and wonderful experience you could imagine. A new understanding of life, relationships, and much more is available **once** you begin making choices outside your comfort zone.

Then think about all the things currently within your comfort zone. Were they always there? Did you do something scary back then, and now you don't blink an eye about it? Think about a time when you were scared to do something; maybe it was asking your current or previous partner out, flirting, or both. You noticed the attraction when you saw them or their picture because you felt a tingle inside. You were interested. You wanted them, and you knew it. Did you feel some hesitation about making the first move? Would you get rejected? Would you be perceived as coming on too strong? Regardless of what uncomfortable thoughts you had, you still took action. You did it because you wanted it badly enough. You were willing to get awkward and uncomfortable to get what and who you wanted.

I was in a relationship with a wonderful woman for just shy of seven years. We met during a time of great transition in both our lives. She was a joyful, brilliant, free spirit, and absolutely gorgeous. As we grew in the relationship, it became clear, sometimes jokingly and sometimes painfully, that we might not be the ones for each other. We simply had different definitions of what partnership looked like. Battling between resentment, love, and loneliness, we had many good and a few bad moments. When we should have exchanged thoughtful gestures, we exchanged hurtful words instead. We had a few breakups but would inevitably end up back together. It was too painful to be with each other and too painful to be without each other.

She was the stronger one and spoke the scary words that started the end of the relationship. I knew we needed to change, but I was unwilling to experience the repercussions, the loneliness, depression, sadness, and fear that would come with the change. She broke up with me twice during our relationship, but I found ways to weasel myself back into her heart. This cycle left us wondering what we were fighting for and why we kept getting back together.

After a particular event, I knew, in my heart, something had to change. My boss invited us to dinner, but I had to leave my girlfriend at home. When I asked her to be ready and dressed appropriately in going-to-the-boss's-house attire my request fell on deaf ears. It was the last straw. It took another letdown—another request unmet for me to finally say my version of the scary words to end the relationship. Shortly after this event, I came home from work and said, "We had to talk."

I was finally willing to get uncomfortable, step outside my comfort zone, and create a new and different experience in my relationship. I was terrified. I had a massive part in why our relationship was the way it was, and here I was, sounding the death knell. We knew our relationship needed to change. I asked if she would be willing to see a couples therapist, and she agreed. We went to a half-dozen sessions, and the result was clear. We ended the relationship in the most loving way possible. We owed that much to each other.

Today my ex and I are each happier apart than we ever were together. I often think about what would have happened if we had just continued our cycle. I know for damn sure I wouldn't be writing this book or married to my wonderful wife. More importantly, I wouldn't know or understand what partnership could be like, what joyful, playful love is, and most importantly, what receiving radical support from my partner looks like.

Get Comfortable Being Uncomfortable

My name is Bob and I'm a recovering addict. I've been addicted to maximum levels of comfort my entire life. I've avoided discomfort like the plague in every life situation possible. Anything but experiencing maximum comfort was going to kill me. It's not entirely abnormal to live life this way. Most people live life this way, and it can be awesome. Their entire existence is built around being as comfortable as possible in their relationships, career, and creative outlets. It's fine and a great way to live; however, if you're experiencing life this way and feel there must be something more, then you have work to do—uncomfortable work.

Before taking a rigorous self-development program and training program to be an ontological coach, I had what most people would consider a fantastic life. Everything one could want. I had access to: an outstanding career with opportunities for growth, a committed relationship with a beautiful woman, a nice condo, a cool car, and a creative outlet. Society told me I should be happy, content, and comfortable. I wasn't. Day by day, I came home from work exhausted to an unfulfilling relationship, which had me wondering if there was more available to me in love and a relationship. I knew there must be.

I did whatever it took just to make it. I was too scared to (*a*) dream bigger, (*b*) be bold, and (*c*) get uncomfortable getting whatever I **truly wanted**. I was more comfortable desiring what I wanted than actually getting uncomfortable with having what I wanted. This comfort kept me in relationships that were going nowhere, causing me to take months, and sometimes years, to get over ex-partners. I was unwilling to get uncomfortable.

When I finally decided to be proactive about my life and relationships, I had to step outside my comfort zone. Getting what you want can be uncomfortable because it requires different, unfamiliar actions. The rub is that everything that's new and possible is in the unknown. Get present with the possibility you can have the relationship you want, but it requires trust, faith, and a hell of a lot of courage.

Tasha contacted me through social media, wanting to know more about coaching. We connected, and I spent an hour talking with her and getting clear about what she wanted. She was such a kind soul. Her voice was caring, and I sensed a deep sadness within. She was telling me the story I shared earlier in this chapter. She knew she needed a change, and there was more opportunity out there for her. She had everything one should want in her life and relationships, yet she yearned for more fulfillment in life.

She wanted a more profound love with a partner who matched her passion, one who was worthy of her brilliance, grace, and beauty. She imagined a fairytale romance and a future worth fighting for. Tasha was faced with a decision to either remain where she was or step out into discomfort. She was uncomfortable investing in herself, her relationship, and her life experience. She created an awareness of what life could be, but she couldn't get past the required investment to work with me, fine. As I reflected on our conversation, I thought perhaps we were talking about her fear. Yes, there was discomfort and anxiety about the investment, but more likely, she had a fear of getting exactly what she wanted. She couldn't quite see that she could create it due to her unwillingness to trust herself. I checked in with her via email from time to time. Her reply to a cheery, "Hey, how's it going?" was met with, "It's okay, I guess."

Choose Your Own Adventure

She chose her it's-okay-I-guess, just-good-enough relationship by not choosing herself. She didn't have to invest in herself or work with me, but would she choose to do any other self-development work? There are a gazillion support structures on the planet to help people with self-development. Choose one. Lean into it fully. Indulge and lick the plate clean.

Not choosing is still a choice. Ultimately, Tasha didn't choose herself, which is the heartbreaking part of my work. Yes, it's uncomfortable, but if you're reading this book, you're uncomfortable in a relationship that probably, maybe, or definitely sucks.

CHAPTER ELEVEN

TAKING CARE OF YOU

> "Happiness is the highest form of health."
> - Dalai Lama

"I don't feel well," Sharon said, "I have no energy, I feel like crap, and I just feel like giving up." Sharon and I were in a discovery session, which are complimentary sessions I offer to prospective clients. Together we figure out what the person wants, what's in the way, and what would be possible if the client could remove those roadblocks, of course, with my help. During these sessions, I also assess whether (*a*) I will let a person hire me, (*b*) I feel I can coach and support them, and (*c*) they're coachable or not. For our coaching relationship to work optimally, we need to be whole and healthy. For every ten people I speak with, my guess is that only one is coachable, a good fit for my practice, and willing to invest the time and money in themselves.

Not everyone is ready or open for this work, and I won't let just anyone hire me, even if they do have the time or money. Like any relationship, the one between a coach and a client must work synergistically and collaboratively to make a meaningful difference. A person's fitness makes up a large part of their readiness and openness to endure this type of self-development. I don't mean fitness in the traditional sense regarding how many push-ups or sit-ups a person can do. I mean physical steadfastness to withstand the additional emotional, spiritual, and mental growth that must take place. I'm not suggesting potential clients are never allowed to have bad feelings and behave as if they're always in a state of Zen, like monks who spend all their time meditating on a mountain. Still, you need to be responsible for your physical, mental, emotional, and spiritual well-being. This type of personal responsibility is a prerequisite to work with me.

With that said, their well-being doesn't have to be perfect either. As a coach, I wouldn't have a job if any aspect of life was perfect. My work is based on people having gaps in their experience of life. I help bridge and close these gaps. So I encourage you to commit to working on your well-being because it's the foundation for all your future growth. Again, your well-being doesn't have to be perfect or at any specific level. Experiencing challenges and taking appropriate action is the foundation for a successful relationship and a co-creative future between a coach and the client. If there's a breakdown in your health and well-being, working to become well can be challenging. Be willing to overcome these breakdowns before or during our time working together. You'll be more empowered, and the results will happen quicker.

Sharon was willing to explore how her well-being impacted her ability to show up for life; this exploration wasn't only for herself but also for her desire to have a better relationship with her wife. She struggled with having the energy and time to deepen the connection in her marriage. She and her partner knew they needed a change, but they both were unsure how to proceed. It was clear the place to start was working on Sharon's relationship to her own well-being. How we empower our well-being is an expression of how we love ourselves or not. My belief, training, and experience have shown that it's challenging to build and create vibrant, loving relationships on top of a weak well-being foundation.

Building a life and relationship that dreams are made of requires a sound footing. Imagine building a house on a foundation of sand. It won't end up well. Building a good relationship on top of feeling unwell in all aspects of life also won't end up well.

Ultimately, Sharon could not create this deep connection when she felt exhausted. She couldn't see past her physical complaints, nor was she willing to mend them first. Sadly, this excluded her from my practice, and I didn't work with her. She wanted to immediately work on fixing her marriage, but I felt strongly she needed to care for herself and her well-being first. Build a foundation first, and the rest will follow. Usually, we work on these at the same time, but the connection wasn't being made, so we moved on from each other.

Sharon and I co-created some practices she could explore to support her well-being. We also created several new ways of **being** and **doing** to practice in her relationship. She didn't have the energy to commit to our coaching, which was okay. Maybe she needed to experience more breakdowns, emotional pain, and a lack of fulfillment. I'll be here when she's ready.

Can You Be Natural?

I'm not a health expert. Since I'm not trained in that area, I don't know what you specifically need to take care of yourself. I do, however, share with my clients that they're the experts on their well-being because, deep down, they know what they need, but they just forget how to listen.

Your body, mind, heart, and gut provide signals about what you need. Many people become so disconnected from their inner well-being they become confused and bewildered once they realize they lack energy and feel like shit. Your body is meant to feel good and be energized and powerful. If you lack energy and feel crappy, then **your symptoms** are your well-being, telling you that you need attention and nurturing. If you don't feel energized and powerful most days, there is work to do on your foundational well-being.

A crucial element of establishing a solid foundation for your well-being is to determine whether you're in process with a general state of health or sickness. Being in process means you're an active contributor to creating a healthy life experience. Since being in process with your health and well-being is your natural state as a human, you're **meant** to actively create your well-being. You work to move the needle every day. Your body's natural state is one of wanting to be healthy. Just ask. Your body is constantly healing itself and letting you know what it needs, likes and doesn't like. Your job, as the inhabitant of your body, is to listen and respect its voice. Ever heard, "Your body is your temple"? You'll suffer if you've sacrificed your health as many do to commitments like work, kids, errands, and significant others. You must come first. If not, then all other relationships will suffer.

Beware! The list of excuses and circumstances is exhaustive. And the excuses and circumstances mentioned in this list can endlessly continue as you find a million reasons not to take care of yourself. Maybe you don't eat what you know is healthy, exercise, move your body as it wants to be moved, or get appropriate rest to nurture yourself. Well, if you don't use it…you lose it.

It's a fact that there are many ways you can sabotage your well-being. Some of these ways include: (*a*) holding on to words that you need to say aloud, (*b*) tolerating something that doesn't serve you, or (*c*) stopping the work to achieve a goal or dream. How do some people seem to do it all while others can't avoid hitting the snooze button fifteen times before falling out of bed? There will always be a reason. Love yourself. Be the reason why you achieve the goals you want. You're worth it, and it's in service to the relationship that you want with yourself and others.

It's Really (Just) Self-Love

Well-being starts with love—self-love. Explore if your self-love can inspire you to take the following actions:

- ◆ Make the difference you want in your life and relationships.
- ◆ Pass up the food and drink that doesn't serve you.
- ◆ Get up an hour early to exercise before your day takes off.
- ◆ Go to bed at a reasonable time and get eight to nine hours of sleep.
- ◆ Get professional support from a coach, trainer, or therapist.
- ◆ Invest in yourself and your life.

Are you worth it? If you are, when will you start? Relating to yourself as the generator of love you want in your life must begin with you. Yes, the old cliché "How can you love another if you don't love yourself?" is true. Start by noticing how you love your body. What are the loving actions you do for it? In my journey, this question became a powerful indicator and an opportunity to notice who I was with myself.

"Is This Loving Myself?"

I was fat, sick, and tired. I had no energy, and everything felt like a nuisance. Pushing three hundred pounds, I was dangerously close to becoming diabetic and just about ready to buy the next size up again in all my clothing until I had an epiphany one day—I didn't love myself! Really! How did I love myself? Let me share some ways I discovered this. I was

- Not drinking enough water,
- Eating an entire pizza and pint of ice cream in one sitting,
- Generally eating things I knew would make me feel awful,
- Not going to the gym across the street from my home,
- Not asking for help,
- Not taking on my therapeutic healing work,
- Staying up late to watch dark, violent TV shows,
- Not giving a shit about my commitments,
- Convincing myself I didn't give a shit about my commitments,
- Lying to myself about being healthier than I was, and
- Not getting my needs met in my relationship.

Be intentional with your well-being, a.k.a. self-love. Choose it every day and make small steps toward it. Only you can define what self-love is. Create your definition and practice it.

When I started my journey into self-love, it was a conversation with myself. I had to earn self-love. I earned it by going to the gym, eating well, and behaving in the **right ways**. Guess what? It was never enough. I never wanted to do it because I knew it wouldn't be enough. I was bound to fail and have evidence of failure. Nonsense, right?

Approaching self-love this way was a losing battle for me. It never was enough. I didn't work out hard enough, eat well enough, or behave the right way. I wasn't choosing to love myself even when I thought I had taken the **necessary actions**. This approach to self-love wasn't working.

During my coach training program, a huge revelation came to me. Each year, I got one or two participants to mentor, coach, and train in my leadership development program. That year, I was assigned to mentor five people. On top of my full coaching practice, getting to mentor, train, and coach five additional humans was asking a lot. How the hell would I keep up with mentoring and be effective and impactful with my mentees and clients, family, friends, team, **and** marriage? Like—what the hell? Can you imagine how overwhelmed and busy I was?

Consider a time in your life when your day-to-day demands gave you plenty of excuses not to address your health and well-being. It was the perfect storm. I was going down fast, putting myself last, and not doing what I knew I should care for myself.

The revelation came in a conversation with my coach. It was one of those breakthrough, holy-shit-my-life-will-never-be-the-same conversations that often happen in coaching. We were looking at my earnings conversation. Since I couldn't earn self-love by doing the right actions, I became consistently overwhelmed and exhausted, a hot mess from Bummerville.

Then, the aha moment came. Instead of earning self-love by taking care of myself, what if I did it because I chose self-love? I began asking myself that question multiple times each day. It was a simple but profound shift. You're invited to practice it and ask yourself the question, "Is this behavior me loving myself?"

I began noticing how often I didn't love myself. A lack of self-love was rampant everywhere. It showed up in my thoughts, feelings, conversations I had with myself, and day-to-day actions in life. Once I began assessing those thoughts, feelings, and actions against this simple question, I found many ways I didn't love myself. Those ways included:

◆ Thinking negative thoughts,
◆ Not getting enough sleep,
◆ Eating poorly,
◆ Staying isolated,
◆ Not being vulnerable and sharing honest feelings, and
◆ Not taking vitamins.

It was rampant. Asking this simple yet profound question created a foundation to have a different, productive conversation and approach to how I loved myself. It was like someone ripped off the blindfold, and I saw life with a new set of eyes. I developed power where there was none before. I began feeling more and more alive. Then the ultimate awareness and act of self-love happened.

I loved working out, losing weight, eating better, and becoming a madman. Caring for myself was no longer a chore but a choice and a practice. I was having fun. I practiced every day and got terrific results.

I felt better, looked better, my head was clearer, my heart was more open, and I was willing to do bigger, scarier actions in to accomplish my goals.

One day while running on the treadmill at the gym, I was tired, sore, and just not feeling it. I asked myself, "Is this loving myself, Bob?" Like a lightning bolt, the answer was, **No!** I wasn't loving myself at the gym, working out, and exercising that day.

What? It wasn't. That day the most loving thing I could've done for myself was to (*a*) rest, (*b*) take a break, (*c*) eat some good food, (*d*) drink water, and (*e*) relax.

This was a groundbreaking awareness. After a lifetime of earning self-love by going to the gym, eating right, and behaving the right ways, I got to practice loving myself and giving my body exactly what it **needed**—rest—and not what I **thought** it should, could, or would need if I blah blah blah. That morning I practiced self-love in a totally different way from before. I trusted myself, knowing what I truly needed.

Your Body Is Your Temple

If you don't take care of your body, then where will you live? Seriously, where will you live if your body is unhealthy? This becomes more significant as I become older and more daring in life and business. I'm clear every day about what to do and, more importantly, what not to do to keep my body healthy enough to make the difference I want in my life and the lives of others. Taking care of yourself is one of the most beneficial practices you can do for your relationship with yourself and relationships with others. I'm not an expert on health and don't know what you should do from a nutritional or exercise standpoint, but for you to be the best version of yourself, it requires taking exquisite care of yourself. If you need a little education in this arena, here it is: eat whole foods and less food. Move your body more. That's what I can offer you. I'm not a doctor, nutritionist, or exercise physiologist. Follow their advice if you have one or all of these professionals in your corner.

Health Is Wealth

Where you're at in your journey to take care of your well-being will dictate how well you show up in your relationships. If you feel like crap, you'll eventually feel like crap in your relationship. If you're exhausted and overwhelmed, you'll blow off dates, not respond to calls and texts, and feel resigned. These actions will impact the quality of your life and how you experience relationships. You'll stay home and be isolated, sitting on the couch. You'll perpetuate the cycle by eating crap and not moving in ways that support you. That cycle will also impact how you create your life and relationships. If you want a healthy, loving relationship with someone, then create it with yourself first.

I included this chapter for a specific reason. Your health and well-being are the foundation for everything you'll create in your life. Think about it. When you've felt great, what was your experience of life and relationships like? When you felt like crap, what was going on in your life and relationships? There may be a chicken-or-the-egg effect, but when you feel better, you have more access to what you want. That's because you have access to power. Having more power means having more of everything you want. You'll have the energy to show up as you want. You'll be grounded in your body, your head will be clear, you'll have confidence, and your heart will be freer and more open. Vulnerability will be an inviting challenge versus a death sentence.

Assessment Time

Honestly and authentically review how well you've been taking care of yourself. Warning: this review can become a shame spiral. Using this process as a weapon against yourself is easy, so be forewarned. This isn't where you want to **should on yourself**. The would've-could've-should've narrative needs to be removed from your vocabulary. You're 100 percent responsible for your well-being. Got it? So, if you **would, could, and should** on yourself, then you chose that. Stop **shoulding** on yourself.

Choosing what supports, sources, nourishes and heals you is worth it. You're worth choosing well-being as an act of self-love and practicing it a little every day. Seriously, just practice it. How well are you taking care of yourself? Physically, emotionally, mentally, and spiritually, what actions are you reliably and consistently taking? Where do you let yourself off of the hook? Where do you excel? What next level would support you in creating the life and relationship of your dreams? Create a list of areas in your life impacted by your health and well-being status. Here are some areas of your life to consider:

- Physical health
- Emotional health
- Mental health
- Spiritual health
- Productivity in life and work
- Sexual health
- All your relationships (past, present, future, self, others, romance, career)
- Add whatever else

What do you notice? Are there areas of your life that need additional support and structure? Are there areas where you're killing it? Was there a time when all was well, and something happened? Create a deeper level of understanding. Practice one or two action items with awareness in each area. Start small. Awareness paired with action will generate results.

Start Slow!

The killer of progress is motivation. Read that again. We typically start something new because we're motivated to change. Think about your last New Year's resolution. You emptied the fridge and pantry of all the bad food and bought more vegetables than you have in months—maybe years. You were full of pride and excitement in the checkout lane at the grocery store with a bounty of leafy greens and colorful, healthy food. You even bought a bunch of kale. You signed up for a killer deal at the gym—maybe even hired a personal trainer. You got a gift certificate to the yoga studio, bought new gym clothes, or signed up again at that place to watch your weight and called a buddy to hold you accountable. You did everything. You were all in!

You were super motivated. Then mid-January rolled around, and one day you woke up and didn't feel like it. You wanted a nice feeling and an admirable goal. What we know about feelings is they never, ever, **ever** last. Have you ever been happy, sad, or excited forever? Nope. So why would you stay motivated forever? Another change, desire, or dream is killed by motivation. Look at your goal with a new lens. See your goals in a way that doesn't depend on motivation; find a way to support yourself when the I-don't-feel-like-it moment inevitably shows up. Motivation is a good start, but it won't sustain you.

Instead of relying on motivation, which comes and goes, practice choice. Practice commitment. Practicing having a big and scary goal requires an uncomfortable amount of accountability. Build on small wins and create powerful, sustaining habits. Practice going one percent further from where you usually stop. Find something joyful, fun, and exciting for you. Be with whatever comes up for you. Notice where you start and stop making progress, embrace your new awareness, intentionally choose, and practice moving toward a solid foundation of health and well-being.

Consider your well-being as a journey. You'll never arrive at your destination of health and well-being. There will always be more to explore, discover, choose, and practice. It's an evolution. You're also creating the best version **of** yourself—**for** yourself. You're also choosing it for the version of yourself that will show up in the relationship of your dreams coming soon. Be easy, go gently, and never, ever, ever give up. This is you loving yourself, and you're so worth it. Right?

CHAPTER TWELVE

COURAGE AND HEART

> "It takes courage to grow up and become who you really are."
> - E.E. Cummings

It takes courage to create the relationship of your dreams while standing in the fear, loneliness, confusion, waiting, wanting, and potential, knowing you could experience the almost inevitable heartbreak that comes with this journey. It takes courage to face the fact that what you have now may not be what you want, or doesn't honor what your heart **truly desires**. It's terrifying to look at your partner and realize they aren't the one, or to look in the mirror, see your sadness and know you must change.

It takes courage to take yourself on. It takes courage to stand firm in wanting to receive love the way you want to give it and demand the experience of love and life you want. If you haven't acknowledged yourself for that, do it now. Coming to the awareness that you want and deserve more and better is a big deal. Waking up each day to reinvent yourself as you birth an extraordinary relationship is astonishing. It's entirely unreasonable. You're in the highly irrational process of designing exactly what you want. It's audacious. So take a moment to acknowledge yourself. Take a deep breath in and hold it for a few seconds. Feel yourself in your body. Celebrate yourself and what you're creating. Nice work!

What is courage? Here's what it's not: courage is not fearlessness. Clients often tell me how afraid they are. They speak about fear as if it's terrible and there's something wrong with being afraid. Fear is simple. Fear is information—period. That's it. Is your fear asking you to do something? Is it asking you to push into the uncomfortable unknown? Is it demanding you open up something that's been closed for a long time, or go where you know your heart calls you? Courage isn't an absence of fear. Courage is much more.

Fear Is Information

Imagine you're the protector of your village tucked high in the rolling countryside, surrounded by beautiful hills, rock outcroppings, wild grass prairies, and lush green forests. Your identity is deeply embedded in your village. You've lived there your entire life. You're fully invested in its safety and security. You're a sorceress, goddess, angel, wizard, knight, cleric, or maybe even a bard. Choose an image of a warrior you can identify with and have fun.

The village you've lived in and helped protect your whole life is thriving and abundant. Each day the market is full of goods, and the blacksmith makes tools to help construct new buildings popping up everywhere. The farmer brings in her crops and livestock. Tailors and cobblers clothe the entire town in beautiful, rich garments. All the townspeople are thriving. Life is good. The village is a beehive of activity, getting ready for the huge fair happening in two days to celebrate the harvest.

That evening the sun casts an amber hue overall. The last minutes of the warm sun's rays hit your face as a smile moves across your lips. You can't help but think about how good life is for you. As you turn to head home, you hear it; an awful, piercing sound that sends shivers through your total being. It's a deafening screech from the east. You don't want to believe it, but you know it can only mean your worst fear is coming true. It's a familiar yet blood-curdling, unwelcome sound. As much as you don't want to believe it, you know exactly what the sound is and where it's coming from.

It's the dragon. The ferocious dragon has terrorized your village throughout your lifetime. Its destruction and mayhem have called you forth so you became the village protector. The same dragon killed your family ten years prior by eating and flying away with everyone you loved.

It's a monster, the epitome of evil, and a killer of possibility. Years ago, village citizens chased the dragon away into the mountains. Finally, all was thought to be safe. Everyone believed the dragon was gone for good, but it has returned.

What do you think is happening to you as the village protector? What are you feeling? What are you noticing? What thoughts do you have to be with? What's happening in your body?

The history of this dragon and the devastation it brings is terrifying. What will you do as the village protector? Do you run or stay and fight?

You have a duty, and the people of the village count on you. Therefore, you hold fast to the vital role as the village protector. Now you're being called into action. What do you choose? It may not always feel like it, but you still have a choice. Do you run toward the dragon with a sword and shield in hand? Or do you run away from the dragon as fast as you can? You have a choice. In the moment, what do you need to help you choose how you'll act? Will it be your commitment, sense of duty, and agreement to support the village because you said that you'd be there no matter what came to attack the village? Action is **required now.** What will you do?

Thanks for letting me geek out on Dungeons and Dragons for a moment. For those who don't know, Dungeons and Dragons is a fantasy role-playing game where a hero typically defeats the dragon. I realize it's not everyone's type of story. The story may not resonate with you entirely, but I use it to illustrate an important point: we can choose to let fear run our lives. Most people recoil from fear, like they avoid touching a hot flame. Even if you're (1) afraid that something may be wrong, (2) convinced there's something to avoid, or (3) tempted to move away from your discomfort and go back to your comfort zone again. You'll **still be** required to step through your fear so you can create your next relationship—guaranteed. Remember, fear is just information. What you do or don't do with the information makes the difference.

Be courageous **in the face of fear.** The definition of courage is acting even when you're afraid. It's not about waiting to be unafraid and then acting. So as the protector, handling that dragon is terrifying, right? But as the protector, you're called by purpose and committed to doing it anyway. Do what you must in the face of your fears.

What are your proverbial relationship dragons? These are the feelings and actions you've been avoiding in your life and relationships because you find them terrifying. Discover what's there for you to process, heal, forgive, accept, and work on. Is it a broken heart you won't allow to heal; a sick body you haven't committed to getting healthy; or holding on to emotional pain and resisting forgiveness for yourself, others, or any experience from the past?

Be willing to slay or tame your dragons. Without addressing them, they tend to return with increasing intensity, ferocity, and a greater capacity for destruction. Run toward the fear and not away from it. Deal?

Now is an excellent time to list your personal relationship dragons. You can start by asking yourself the following questions:

◆ What are you afraid of?
◆ What information are you receiving from your fear?
◆ What would help you to act although you're afraid?
◆ What's on the other side of your fear?
◆ Do you notice a pattern to your fear?

Courage to Change

It takes courage to change. Whether it's your current circumstances or how you interpret and hold those circumstances, courage will be required. Back then, coming home to my girlfriend of seven years and asking her to have a serious conversation was terrifying. The talk itself wasn't scary, but the consequences of it were frightening. I knew it meant change, and many things would be different. I would be alone. I would have no one to come home to at the end of the day. It meant being confronted by my emotions, role in the relationship, judgments, and interpretations.

When you have an opportunity to have a difficult conversation, what typically happens? You talk yourself out of it. You convince yourself that things aren't so bad and will get better. You get distracted with life and forget. The pattern is repeated over and over until one of two things happens. You give up or create such a mess the relationship explodes dramatically. Kicking the can down the road on what you truly want comes at a cost. Over time, you'll grow unhappy, resentful, resigned, bitter, and convinced that what you want is impossible.

Mindset

Your mindset is one of the most powerful tools to create what you want. How you choose to think directly impacts what's possible. If you think it won't work or will never happen, guess what?—it probably won't happen. Conversely, if you're open to the process and curious while believing it's possible for you and acting in service of that possibility (even when you feel scared), guess what?—it probably will happen.

Could it be that simple? Ask anyone you admire who has what you want how their success started. It likely began with the thought, "I can do this!" Start believing the relationship you want is possible.

This will take practice. Our brain and subconscious mind tend to be sneaky. It constantly tries to keep you safe. This survival trait is overused in the quest for love. You build a wall, close your heart, or give up. These are ways that we try to protect ourselves by playing it safe. Playing it safe isn't entirely wrong, but if it keeps you from getting what your heart yearns for, then it's worth exploring.

Remember the discussion about your comfort zone from Chapter Ten? Your comfort zone wants you to stay comfortable. You know everything inside it and what will and won't happen. Closing your heart and building a wall around your emotions could be your comfort zone. You stay safe and protected; everything is predictable, and no one—I mean no one—can hurt you again. It's comfortable, right?

So what happens when your comfort comes at the cost of what you want? You may pay this cost in every facet of your life, such as your relationships, finances, and investments in your career, health, or self. Usually, growth is uncomfortable. It requires you to act in ways that you haven't previously acted. It will feel awkward not to act in the typical ways you've always acted. All these feelings are normal responses to taking different actions. This is precisely why you'll want to practice stepping outside your comfort zone. New results require new actions, and nothing changes if nothing is changed.

What would it look like if you stepped outside your comfort zone for your relationships? Yes, it'll be uncomfortable. Practice sharing your honest feelings by asking for what you truly want—what you yearn for. Practice getting comfortable with being uncomfortable. Here are some suggestions to consider:

- ◆ Make the first move.
- ◆ Swipe right on the person who is out of your league.
- ◆ Say, "I love you," first.
- ◆ Get clear and share your next level of commitment.
- ◆ Post on social media that you're single and want an introduction.
- ◆ Don't have sex on the first date.
- ◆ Have sex on the first date.
- ◆ Hire a coach.
- ◆ Hire a matchmaker.
- ◆ Go one percent further than where you usually go.

Slay the Dragon

One of the first opportunities you'll have to practice stepping outside your comfort zone is facing your dragon. That may be a big ask, but what are you here for? Go all in. Run toward the dragon and practice doing what's necessary to kill or tame your relationship dragons. In my experience, the dragon never completely disappears; however, you can gradually build a relationship with your dragons and tame them. I've seen clients experience massive breakthroughs where the issues that made their relationships a hot mess are no longer an issue. Poof! They've been removed. Anything is possible, right?

Don't be surprised when your dragon returns. It's a matter of when it comes back and not if it will come back. When it does, your job is to notice, welcome, face, and love it and to continue moving courageously toward what you want.

Here's a framework to help you name your D.R.A.G.O.N.:

D - Discontent

Notice the discontent. What are you unhappy with? Look everywhere, practice courage, and have tough conversations with yourself. What must be said?

R - Release

How can you release the discontent and wipe the slate clean? Practice forgiveness and the freedom that comes with letting go.

A - Anxiety

What anxiety must be addressed? Do you need additional help and support to slay your dragons? Many support professionals are available to guide and love you.

G - Grief

Are you still recovering from a painful, traumatic episode? Do you need more time, help, support, or love? Are you trying to rush the process and jump in when you aren't truly ready? Honor the process. Your future self will thank you.

O - Obstacles

What obstacles are in your way? List them and practice removing them every day. I recommend working with a coach to get beyond what's been in your way for years.

N - New life/love

Once your dragon is slayed, it grants access to a new experience of life and love. I battle my dragon most days, and I have the tools and people in my life to support and help me. I've created an extraordinary life and one I'm so grateful to enjoy. You can create it too.

Discomfort Is a Gift

Courage is uncomfortable. Remember a time when you had to muster up your courage? There are many moments in life when fear and discomfort lead you to stop, change course, or at least take a moment to pause. Did you summon your courage during:

- ◆ A job interview;
- ◆ A first date;
- ◆ Signing up for a race;
- ◆ Hiring a coach;
- ◆ Hiring a personal trainer;
- ◆ Making a substantial financial investment;
- ◆ Saying, "I do."; or
- ◆ Jumping off the diving board into the pool?

Notice that discomfort, combined with some spectrum of fear, usually precedes an act of courage. Your pain and anxiety are precisely where you stopped or gave up in the past. It's okay to stop and pause; however, we're in the business of creating new outcomes, remember? So walk through your discomfort and fear on your way to the relationship you want.

Feeling uncomfortable is natural when you confront new and unpredictable experiences. This discomfort is designed to keep you safe and protected, causing you to slink back to your comfort zone. Remember, everyone likes their safe, predictable comfort zone because it doesn't require action in the presence of fear. Your comfort zone normalizes your process of recoiling to slink back into it, so you ultimately stop and give up. Your new awareness will provide the insight to choose and act differently leading you to what you genuinely want.

Keep it simple:

◆ The comfort zone is everything you know to say, do, or create with predictable results or a lack of new results; and

◆ Outside your comfort zone is entirely unknown, unpredictable, and scary, with endless possibilities or an abundance of new results.

Saying, "I Do"?

I remember the exact moment when I faced my fear. My wife and I were in our early courtship stage. We were on our second date, and I kept hearing a silent voice say, "There she is," meaning the woman I was waiting to meet was finally here. All the terrible dates, online dating zoo of messages, broken hearts, and lonely nights led me to that moment. Shona sat on the couch in my condo, and I stood in the kitchen looking at her. "There she is," the voice said again.

"There she is," and there was also a **big** "but." Could I be sure? Could I risk another broken heart? Could I live with the consequences of committing to one woman? Would I be happy with one woman? Could I be okay telling the other women I was dating that I met **the one**?

These thoughts flowed through my mind like a river of confusion. Here was everything I wanted, and I was scared, uncomfortable, and felt more confused by the moment. While my head and heart were swirling in a pit of discord, something divine happened as if a bolt of lightning had hit me. Everything became clear as all my self-development work and training came to the forefront of my mind and heart. I saw what a lifetime of failed relationships taught me.

What became crystal clear was that this river of thoughts and confusion had nothing to do with the other person. More specifically, it had nothing to do with Shona. I was outside my comfort zone. I was catching feelings for this woman. She was everything I ever wanted, and I couldn't believe it. I was terrified of committing to her. Could I be all in and face my fear and discomfort? It was so much to risk, yet I had to risk it to create the level of relationship and love I yearned to experience. Although I was afraid and unsure of the outcome, I had to jump into this opportunity and be willing to get hurt. I overcame the fear and discomfort of being outside my comfort zone and marched courageously toward what I wanted.

I walked toward my dragon and faced it head-on. It made zero sense from a comfort-zone perspective, but I knew the possibilities would be endless if I could do it while I was afraid, choosing to endure the temporary discomfort.

Allowing myself to do it while I was afraid, I proposed to Shona five months later. Instead of fear, I chose courage and opened the door to the most beautiful relationship I've ever known. That wouldn't be possible if I stayed comfortable. The default approach would've been to continue living in the unknown while making no real commitment, as I dated others and chose not to create a future with anyone. It required different actions and beliefs to get what I wanted, which took courage. Practice courage. Face your D.R.A.G.O.N.

CHAPTER THIRTEEN

COME OUT, COME OUT, WHEREVER YOU ARE!

> "Be yourself. Everyone else is taken."
> - Oscar Wilde

If you've made it this far, then I want to congratulate you. Well, not just want—I do congratulate you. It takes courage and a whole heap of truth, and trust to open up to who you truly are and make positive changes. Up to this point, we've been looking at the past, thinking about what's in the way, and taking an earnest, uncomfortable look within. Take a moment to acknowledge yourself. Acknowledge that you're beginning to create the relationship you truly desire. You're developing the relationship you yearn for, which will make a difference in your quality of life.

Reading this book, gaining awareness, and taking action will clear the debris of your past, limiting beliefs, and a known but undesirable future. It will also interrupt the predictability of your path to building relationships. You have made a path for a new foundation. This foundation will be a solid structure to create an intentional partnership and relationship where you give and receive love in a meaningful, impactful way. You'll create a relationship that doesn't suck, not only with the person of your dreams but also with yourself.

When creating anything new, it's crucial to have a vision of who you already are and who you can be in a relationship before moving toward your goal. What will you build on this new foundation? What will you create? How? What will be your measures of progress? How will you course correct if you get blown off the rails?

You'll need to (*a*) get clear on your vision and the values that guide you, (*b*) rediscover your interests, and (*c*) manifest the completion of your goals for love. You'll need to use your innate strength and practice using your natural gifts. The gifts you possess, your vision, and your interests are already within you. They've been there all along. You're a gift simply by being who you are already. Remember, there's no one else exactly like you—no one.

Nice to Meet You

The first few sessions are a rediscovering process in much of the work I do as a coach. You'll be reminded of (*a*) who you already are, (*b*) who you know yourself to be, (*c*) what you know is possible, and (*d*) what you honestly yearn for in your relationships. It may sound a little woo-woo or fluffy, but you'll benefit if you allow yourself to take it in.

Somewhere along the way, life **happened to you.** A failed relationship fucked you up. Add multiple failed relationships, some sabotaging patterns, a little bit of carnage, and a new limiting story, and—voilà!—a wounded persona of you was created. You began losing yourself. You shrank, limited, or disingenuously reinvented yourself to fit in or be liked. Frankly, you did whatever it took to survive.

I don't mean to literally survive unless that was a real experience for you, but you did what you had to do to get the love you craved. This approach probably wasn't always intentional. It neither came from your highest and best expression of yourself nor was it in alignment with your vision for your relationship goals and aspirations. Your approach was likely based on fear, limited possibility, and circumstances. You did what you did to get what you got to meet a need based on scarcity. Phew! You were surviving.

Survival mode isn't necessarily a problem or **the problem**, but it's something to notice and become aware of. You're not free, aware, or able to create when you're struggling to survive or just make it through the day, situation, or relationship. When you're in survival mode, your creativity shuts down, and your permission to explore, be free, and allow life to happen naturally is gone. Done-zo! You lose your authenticity, the ability to connect to yourself, and the ability to yearn for what you want. You'll want to get back to having the relationship you crave. It's time to work on your relationship with yourself.

So ask yourself:

◆ Are you authentically yourself?
◆ Do you permit yourself to fully express your feelings and emotions?
◆ Do you allow all of yourself to be loved?
◆ What would a full expression of yourself create in a relationship?
◆ Are you confused about what the hell any of this even means?

It's okay if you're confused. It's not often we get a chance to look at ourselves honestly, an opportunity to rise above the drama of the past and dare to dream. Has it been a while since you connected with yourself? How long has it been since you felt fully present as the human being, miracle, and gift you are? This is the version of yourself you'll want to practice bringing into your relationships. The word "practice" is essential to note since it requires practice to remember (*a*) who you are, (*b*) what you want, and (*c*) why you're here.

If you could wave a magic wand, what would the most authentic version of yourself create in your next relationship? Most importantly, who would you get **to be** if that magic were alive in your life? It is magical. When you connect to the possibility of who you are and what you want, things line up; it's the law of attraction type stuff. I don't know how or why it works, but it's worth mentioning. There are a lot of books and experts on the law of attraction. When you rediscover yourself and align with your authentic identity, your life begins to shift in wonderful new directions.

Take a moment and become present to yourself. Take a deep breath and put your hand on your heart. Notice how you feel in your body. Notice your thoughts and be with your feelings as they arise. Let your thoughts come and go and become present to your spirit. Get present to yourself. Let some tension release and take another deep breath. Then set this book down and ask yourself who you are. Who are you?

Take a few minutes to just be with that question. So who are you?

Your mind will immediately start explaining who you are by what you do. I'm a teacher, a business owner, a hunter, a cyclist, a coach, a grad student, a nurse, a musician, an artist, a carpenter, and a landscaper. It's a confusing question to answer when you decide not to use what you do to describe who you are. The things you do aren't who you are authentically. Remember this as you try to explain who you are without sharing what you do.

So who are you?

If you don't define yourself by what you do, how do you know who you are? One question I ask potential clients is, "What would you like me to know about you?" This question often results in the experience I described above. The person will share five minutes of all the cool, wonderful, sometimes boring, or sometimes tragic experiences they've had in life, but it still doesn't answer the question. The activities you do aren't who you are —who are you?

Let's explore a bit deeper. Outside all the things you've done, earned, accomplished, failed at, fucked up, and lucked out on—who are you? What is the spirit, soul, ethos, life, and quintessence of you? What's the nature of who you are as you? Remember, there's no other you in the entire universe—so who are you?

You must be something or someone, right? Is this getting a little **out there** for you, so now you're feeling confused about how any of this relates to finding love? Hang in there. I'll tie it all together.

A Little Help

Have you ever been in the company of a cooing, googly-eyed baby? It is bright-eyed, curious, and smiling; everything is new and unique. All an infant knows is to be completely engrossed in the moment of exploring, discovering, and enjoying the wonder of everything around them. A baby is a human in its most authentic form, a being engrossed in its presence. That's who you are.

Yes, you grew up and learned to (*a*) walk, (*b*) feed yourself, (*c*) talk, and (*d*) do algebra—or not. You learned how to feel scared, angry, hurt, resentful, and the messy parts of being human. There's a saying among my coaching circle to remember who you were before life happened to you.

It's so apropos here. That precious, beautiful, complete, and whole human **being** is inside you somewhere, but it's there. You'll find there's a human being full of possibility, wonder, joy, and excitement.

It's the version of yourself before (*a*) life happened, (*b*) a lifetime of sucky relationships messed you up, and (*c*) the circumstances you experienced allowed you to create stories and beliefs about what is and isn't possible.

No, I'm not trying to turn you back into an infant. I'm only pointing to what you were like before you experienced life and created a bunch of stories. There was a part of yourself that was available that's not so readily available now. The time is now to tap back into that part. Tap back into you. At your highest and best, you are whole, complete, sourced, loved, content, and **present**. Living life and creating a relationship from this place opens unlimited, new possibilities.

You'll probably never get all the way there, but it's your job to practice being authentic as you get back into a relationship with the unjaded version of yourself where nothing is wrong. The version of yourself that is simply you. It could be considered a form of enlightenment, elevation, ascension, whatever. But the freedom you'll experience will open your heart in ways you probably haven't experienced since you saw your mother for the first time. This is important, and as I said, I'll tie it together.

Remembering yourself in this way will allow the beauty of your quest for love to emerge. Loving yourself will also allow you to give and receive love in ways you have yet to explore. You'll be free to create the most authentic, vulnerable relationship you've ever experienced. It starts with you. Now you know yourself. This is what we're talking about.

Finding Me

I worked for two and one-half years on my master's degree. It was a lot of effort balancing work, life, and school. I spent Sundays writing fifteen-page papers on international economics and crisis management while running a mock shoe company my classmate colleagues were running into the ground. I was juggling so much: the long days at an intense job, keeping up with managing the house, and a ton of schoolwork. I was up to a lot and near or at capacity most days. That wasn't even the hardest part.

The hardest part was managing those I'm-not-enough feelings. I had and, some days, still have a critical inner voice that says I'm not enough. I believed I'd never be enough and would fail. The busier and more overwhelmed I became, that critical voice became louder and louder. I used to feel it was me, but now I realize it's a part of me activated by fear, scarcity, and a lack of faith.

I remember when I enrolled in the university to pursue my graduate degree. I was excited and pumped. I felt I'd finally have what I needed to show up powerfully at work as a middle manager and Director of Operations. Once had the MBA credentials after my RN-BS (Registered Nurse designation, Bachelor of Science degree), I'd have the clout and credibility to let everyone know I was finally enough.

See! It's my badge of honor! I finally arrived and could be good enough for everyone else. Then an overwhelming thought overwhelmed me.

After a year and one-half into the Master's program, I became present to an insatiable emptiness within. No matter how many credentials followed my name, Robert Joseph Conlin, it would never be enough. I spent an entire lifetime trying to discover who I was based on what I earned, produced, performed, achieved, and did. This led to a successful academic and professional career, but the gaping, ravenous hole inside could never be filled. I remember thinking about what came next after graduate school, and the thought of starting a doctoral program floated in my mind.

Then it hit, what a moment of clarity. It was like a flash of lightning that blazed white hot, so I finally saw what I was doing. I was and still am grateful for that moment. I also remember how confusing, scary, and threatening it felt. I didn't know what came next, but I knew it was time to change the path my life was on. It would never make the difference I yearned for in life and my relationships. I was at another crossroad.

Ouch

I became aware that the primary reason for enrolling in an MBA program was to overcome feelings of inadequacy in boardroom meetings. I didn't have the experience or education to show up powerfully when I shared reports during one-on-one business meetings with C-suite executive officers. I realized it was another way to try and prove who I was to myself and the world.

I started noticing that my not-good-enough story was everywhere. I wasn't smart enough or attended a better university. I didn't have the right clothes, girlfriend, house, car, body, hair, complexion, or voice. Damn! It was everywhere…not enough. Ultimately, I discovered I wasn't good enough anywhere. Indeed, I wasn't showing up powerfully and authentically in relationships. So, of course, they sucked.

Can you relate to this thought or belief? Is there a part of you that believes you're not enough? Many of my clients express some version or belief that they're not enough. It's more common than you think. Conversely, do you think you're too much in life and relationships? Your internal critic is constantly judging and assessing you against others. It measures you up to others, and you almost always fall short. It's all about what they have or don't have and what's wrong with you. We all have that inner critic within. If you just heard a voice say, "I don't have that. Bob is a weirdo." **That's it!** That's the internal critic. Your relationship with it will help you remember who you are. You're you; you aren't that voice and all its criticisms.

I Did it Again

Around this time, I started the training program to become a coach. Admittedly, I signed up for the same I'm-not-enough reasons. Becoming a coach was the next shiny, bauble solution to fix me and all the self-criticism. I'd get a toolbox of tools to support me in being the best me and live my best life (insert eye roll). I was in for a big surprise. I had no idea what was even on the horizon of possibilities. That surprise was me.

The difference in my coach training program, the MBA degree, or any other achievement until this point is that I found myself. I was reintroduced to myself. That may sound funny, or hokey, but it's my truth. The coach training program wasn't about learning and regurgitating knowledge; it was about discovering myself to support others to do the same. It was also kind of brutal. Looking honestly at life and how I was living was challenging. Taking responsibility for my relationships was also challenging. It was one of the most vulnerable, eye-opening experiences of my life. With responsibility came an incredible awareness. I could choose:

◆ How I wanted to show up in relationships;
◆ Who I wanted to be;

- Who I wanted to practice being, to gain what I wanted; and
- Who I wanted to be for myself.

Equal parts of relief and resistance flooded my mind, but I was all in. I dove deep into self-development and discovery. I started seeing (*a*) patterns and the ways I sabotaged relationships out of fear, (*b*) a not-enough attitude, and (*c*) critical judgments and assessments. Ouch, indeed! It sucked to fearlessly and honestly look closely at myself in this way. It also made a 100 percent difference in how I create relationships now and how I give and receive love.

After the first year of radical transformation, being held to my greatness, and allowing the process of self-development to unfold, a miracle was created. I felt alive again. I had a purpose, vitality, and a drive to create a new life worthy of who I am by simply being myself. I deserved love and affection and to give that to myself. I could be free from the bondage of that former critical, inner voice and those not-good-enough feelings. I could explore, be with new people, and create new experiences.

I was me again. I woke up to me before a lifetime of bad relationships ruined me. The path was clear. My purpose was clear. The mission to create strong relationships with courage and heart sprang to life. I was alive and willing to powerfully create whatever came next.

So what did you discover from reading about my journey? Are there doors that were closed that are beginning to open? Are the closed doors now shut even tighter? Why? Give yourself permission to explore who you were before life and relationships happened to you. You'll be amazed at what you discover. Don't overthink it. Just be with yourself. **Be love.**

So who am I? Who I am and know myself to be is a leader full of:

- Levity,
- Heart,
- Brilliance, and
- Authenticity.

---- CHAPTER FOURTEEN ----
WHAT DO YOU WANT?

"And, when you want something, all the universe conspires in helping you to achieve it."
- Paulo Coelho, *The Alchemist*

As you start this chapter, it's incredibly important to note what you want **is not** what you don't want. Sometimes when I speak with potential clients for the first time, the frustration, anger, and heartbreak are intoxicating. They're left surviving their relationship due to the combination of not being seen, heard, or understood and not getting their fundamental or intimate needs met for months or maybe even years. Or worse, they focus on what needs to change in a long, dead relationship vs. what they want. So it is no surprise when I ask some clients what they want. All they can speak about is what they don't want. It's almost like a reflex of the sick and tired, sick of being sick and tired.

"Well, I don't want to argue so much. I'm tired of not being heard. It's like we're roommates, and I'm so exhausted trying to make it work. It shouldn't be this hard," Stacy shared with me. Stacy found me through an online search. She knew she needed to change and was desperately searching the internet when she came across one of my blog posts that resonated with her. She took that bold first step and reached out to get my help and support. My heart broke for Stacy. I knew exactly what she felt: lost, stuck, fed up, over all of it, and resigned. Stacy was in her first relationship after a terrible divorce. She was a caring mother to her two children and a fierce warrior for her family. There was so much sadness in her voice and extraordinarily little hope for a new possibility. Again, she found herself in another unfulfilling relationship where she wasn't getting her needs met. "Thanks for sharing, Stacy," I said, "And if I can ask again, what do you want? What you told me is what you don't want. You told me what you're tired of and what you wish you weren't experiencing in your relationship. So, Stacy, what do you want?"

Getting clarity about what we want in a relationship is one of the essential practices we can create in our quest for love. Yet, most of my clients haven't seriously considered this. Early in relationships, we often allow our true intentions to be swept away or overshadowed by infatuation and lust. We leave them for the sake of convenience and the opportunity to get our needs met for the moment. We allow more red flags than green flags and end up like Stacy. Getting into another unfulfilling relationship was her destiny. Her pattern was to ignore what she wanted by not getting crystal clear about what she wanted. Instead, she settled for what she was getting in her relationship. This pattern left her hurt, resentful, and unfulfilled.

Stacy and I worked together for a few months. I supported her by letting her dare to dream about what she wanted and teaching her how to reclaim her voice in her relationships. Stacy loved her current partner profoundly and was willing to work with her partner to improve their experience. She told me our sessions were the only time she could have an open, unbiased conversation and just say it all. Week after week, we designed practices and actions Stacy would take to bring her partner into the conversation and begin shaping her desired experience. Thankfully, her partner was open, willing, and eager to work on the relationship. This isn't always the case, so I consider Stacy and her partner lucky. Stacy learned to set boundaries and ask for what she needed at the moment. She became eager and open to explore deeper levels of intimacy and honesty with her partner. The last time I connected with her, she and her partner were trying to have another child, their love baby, an unlikely possibility before her transformation through coaching.

The lesson from Stacy's story is to check in with yourself. Aside from how you think your relationship has been or how you think it will be, what do you want from a relationship? What has your heart been yearning for? Are you currently experiencing it? Have you ever experienced what you wanted? Clarity is a powerful tool for manifesting your future partner or transforming your current relationship. I genuinely believe it's the same as placing an order to the Universe that states this is the experience and person I'm available to receive. The quote that starts this chapter alludes to the opportunities that will begin to present themselves once you put your order in. The whole Universe will conspire to make it come to pass.

A Vivid Vision

"What you believe is what you achieve." Ever heard that one? It takes courage to believe you can have what you want concerning love, especially if your heart has been broken over and over again. Perhaps you have a lifetime of proof that you won't be loved in a way that matters to you, and all the evidence you need is there to confirm all your relationships will suck. So now what? This is a dare-to-dream exercise and a call forward to have the audacity to believe that what you want is possible. A powerful tool for manifesting your deepest desires is the combination of a Vivid Vision for your future and clarity about what you want or yearn for.

After my divorce, I found myself in Stacy's shoes. I was repeating another relationship pattern while in a new relationship. I found myself in an unfulfilling relationship and was getting smaller every day. I was repeating the same mistakes and was a terrible partner to the woman I said I loved because my actions didn't match my words. My words didn't match my actions, either. What I was experiencing wasn't what I wanted, yet I honestly couldn't start creating what I wanted because I had no idea what that was.

In my self-development journey, I learned the importance of visioning: acting as if I was already living out the dreams of a future I thought was possible. I'll admit, this seemed stupid—hell—dangerous even. What if it didn't happen? What if this beautiful vision for the love I wanted never came true? Was I an idiot for thinking so—a sucker? Was this a setup for another heartbreak? What I came to believe and ultimately choose was the discomfort of it all. I was uncomfortable with what I already had. So, could I be uncomfortable creating what I wanted? Could I move forward in a way that seemed both foreign and confusing? What did I have to lose? I was uncomfortable anyway, right? I could be uncomfortable staying stuck and stopped, or I could be uncomfortable moving toward what I wanted. What would you choose?

My First One

So I dared to dream and wrote my first relationship vision. Support from my coach at the time helped me get clear on the experience I wanted not only with my future partner but also how I experienced myself with that partner. I remember writing this feeling as if it was a bit silly, but I trusted the process. Again! Dare to dream. Here it is:

> Relationship Project - to create the experience of being in a loving partnership where I use my voice, source myself, and I matter. I show up as the kind, loving man I am. I'm open to receiving all her love. I have compassion for myself and communicate understanding from trust and empathy with my partner. My self-compassion gives me a voice to create the experience of home. I co-create my headquarters for all my success and outward expression inside this relationship. This relationship is my foundation and launchpad for everything. There is play, fun, and adventure in our partnership. I'm in a state of relaxation and enjoyment as I appreciate the depth of intimacy. My partner and I facilitate each other's healing, loving, and growth.

In addition to writing the vision and experience, the next important aspect is to declare a date by which you want this vision to come alive in your life. You create both the image and date for this to be successful. I couldn't believe I went on the first date with my future wife two weeks after I wrote this (on October 15, 2017).

My gut intuition knew it was her. Yet I still questioned if it was possible that I met her. Could visioning and declaration be that powerful? All sorts of feelings came. My heartbreaks of the past came back to haunt and protect me. It didn't make sense. I couldn't understand how this was happening. Could it be that easy? My gut knew. There she was. Notice if you start experiencing resistance declaring a date. Resistance is normal. You've probably never looked at creating a relationship the way you create any other goal. Setting a vision and a date it should be complete seems weird with love, right? So notice the resistance not only to creating your future vision but also to declare a date the experience will unfold. Do it anyway.

Goals require a date you will achieve them. Think back to previous goals you've set. Perhaps it was earning your degree or getting into a professional trade. You saw a vision for yourself, so you enrolled in the school and set the date you'd achieve your goal. Maybe you're like me and you set a recurring annual goal to improve your well-being by dropping those holiday pounds by spring. So why don't we set goals regarding love and relationships? If you have a goal of creating this amazing relationship, why would this be any different?

I find that many people stop. They get stuck, and flat-out refuse to declare a date for their relationship to start. They think, "What if the date comes and goes, and I don't have what I said I wanted? Then what? Will it feed into thinking, "Yes, I've failed and can't have what I want!"? This is resistance. This is what keeps you from creating a different experience in your relationships. The I-know-how-it-is-going-to-go-or-should-go belief is preventing you from getting what you want. So if the date comes and goes and you don't get what you want, what will you do? Declare it as a failure and give up? There's more to come on this later. So why make this declaration in the first place? It's simple.

Once you have clarity about what you want with a declared date, it creates velocity and directs your new behavior. I firmly believe it lets the Universe/God/Spirit, or whatever you call it, know you're ready. You're welcoming this experience and person into your life, and the velocity of what you're creating begins to unfold. New people, circumstances, and serendipity will show up in your life. Can I prove this? No. Can I guarantee this? No, but I've seen countless examples with clients with every type of goal imaginable—money, new jobs, better health, and love—all come to fruition.

For instance, Harper, a longstanding client, receives coaching and support to cultivate her self-love. She had a big breakthrough when she chose to leave a romantic relationship that wasn't serving her. Week after week, our calls were dissecting the drama that unfolded in her relationship and getting her reconnected to what she wanted—her vivid vision. As time went by, it was clear what she wanted, her vivid vision wasn't possible with her current partner, despite being madly in love. She finally decided to end the relationship, although it was uncomfortable.

I asked her when she wanted to end the relationship and when she wanted to be in the relationship that she wanted, essentially setting dates for the ending of her current relationship and the beginning of her next one. Yes, the old uncomfortable feelings came up for Harper with declaring a date to end a relationship and finding her love. But she did it anyway. She courageously ended the relationship that wasn't serving her after realizing that what she wanted wasn't possible with her current partner. It was a heartbreaker but a necessary step to move forward. Time passed, and the date she declared for the start of her new relationship was getting closer. Suddenly, a good friend invited her to a Thanksgiving dinner, where a man who was a last-minute add-on guest attended. This man she didn't know walked in, and **boom**—fireworks! What if I told you this happened just a few days shy of her declaration date? They are **still happily together**. Magic, right? I couldn't make it up if I tried.

With a date declared, the Universe will conspire to create the circumstances and possibilities. I believe this. Lean into this belief and keep an open mind and heart. Even with goals outside of a romantic relationship, I've witnessed this phenomenon with most of my clients. I've personally experienced it as well. Whenever I'm stuck on a project or a goal, I go back to visioning and declaration. Finding my partner, purchasing our home in a crazy competitive Chicago housing market, getting pregnant, almost losing our son, then having the healthiest baby we could imagine were all positively impacted by this approach. Time and time again, the gift of getting clear about what you want and when you want it has created miracles.

Take Uncomfortable Action for Love

Getting what you want is not all mystical, magical, and supernatural; it requires hard work. It will require action in the face of fear and discomfort as you move further outside your comfort zone. Declaring a date encourages the behavioral changes you need to make to create what you want. Harper knew she was going to end her unfulfilling relationship by her declared date. Ending that relationship would require her to move into uncomfortable action. She knew that she'd have to have **the conversation**—the it's-over conversation. She knew she would need extra support from friends and family as she began healing. So she enlisted friends to come over and be with her. Harper recommitted to her hobbies and doubled down on aligning her life with the vision she created. Her deadline made her responsible to get what she needed to love herself through her discomfort. It allowed her to take uncomfortable actions. Most people don't think it's a loving act to do the uncomfortable action with the aim of getting what we want. It absolutely sucks to go through a breakup or one more crappy date or get your heart broken one more time. It will be uncomfortable to keep going when you have all the evidence you need to prove it won't work. It will also be uncomfortable when every fiber of your being screams at you to stop.

Declaring a specific result by a specific date will apply to you if you're seeking the love you want. If you know by a specific date, you'll create the relationship you've been yearning for, who do you need to be to create it? What do you need to do? How many dates will you need to go on to find the one? Will you have to clean up some old relationship wreckage or finally call it quits with your friends with benefits? Would you need to (a) get some support for that childhood trauma, (b) hire that coach, (c) get back on the dating apps, or (d) tell the world you're back out there? The declaration calls forth new possibilities and action from a new place of being and doing.

To achieve the declaration you stated to the Universe; you'll need to be in sufficient action to generate the results you want. After reviewing your relationship experiences, can you honestly say that you've:

◆ Acted sufficiently to generate the results you want?
◆ Been 100 percent responsible to create those results?
◆ Been all in, or did you get discouraged and quit?
◆ Had a terrible date, so you convinced yourself to give up?
◆ Repeatedly keep getting the same results?

How have you shown up during the process? Is it a pattern? What message are you giving the Universe? Can you start by taking your power back and declaring and fulfilling the love waiting for you? The power to transform your relationships remains within.

I Still Didn't Find Love

So what happens when you create the clarity and declaration of when you'll find the love of your life, but the date comes and goes? It didn't work out, right? Is Bob full of it? Perhaps you convinced yourself just a bit more that you're unlovable and that what you want is impossible. "You see, I did everything the right way, and I still didn't get the result I wanted." Does that sound like something you'd do? Many of us seek evidence to quit when things get uncomfortable, or we don't get what we want. It's normal to stop doing stuff that doesn't work. It's survival. This is when many of us give up, and you know what happens when you do that. So don't give up, okay?

I assume you're reading this book because your relationship experiences haven't worked. Remember, this is about doing something different to get a different result. So if you'd typically quit, find the evidence to give up, or tell me I'm full of it, then what's something different you can do instead? Take a moment to think and feel in your heart and body. What would come next? When it doesn't go your way, what do you do?

What you do next is simple. **Make a brand-new declaration.** Then review your vision.

Does it still align with what you want and what your heart yearns for? Does it still make you feel good? Are you excited to act? If yes, great! If not, it's time to revise your vision and adjust as necessary to completely embody yourself in the creation of your future relationships. Next, pick a new date. Keep it simple. What's a date that seems like a stretch but doesn't let you off the hook? Your intuition will guide you.

The most important thing you can do is take an honest inventory of your actions. Were you sufficiently being and doing activities to generate what you wanted? Was your mind in a constant battle over how impossible it seemed to meet your person over the next few months **or** how this process seemed to be—well—**too much** of a process and should have been more spontaneous or magical? Did you meet your ideal partner and only go on one date? Did you still invest time and energy in a relationship with an ex you know is going nowhere because you were lonely or horny? Or were you full of possibility every day, putting yourself out there and keeping an open heart and mind because you were reviewing your vision and taking inspired action? Taking this inventory will help you adjust your actions accordingly. Again, are you sufficiently acting to generate the result you want? If you have yet to achieve the result, then it is likely that you haven't been. Get reconnected. Get clear. And declare a new date for the result that you want. Your future self will love you for it.

This chapter was about getting so clear about what you want there's no doubt you're creating it. It's about taking uncomfortable, consistent action to create love the way you've been yearning for it. Plus, making a bold declaration in the face of fear and evidence from the past. Then daring to dream this relationship is possible. Willingness is key. Will you start today?

CHAPTER FIFTEEN

FINDING YOUR PERSON

> "You don't find a lover; you create them inside of your heart."
> - Debasish Mridha

If you haven't found your person, you're looking in the wrong places—those familiar, comfortable, but **wrong** places. If you're willing, then is it time for a new approach? New adventures, experiences, and discoveries await you if you're committed to doing whatever it takes to find your person. If this sounds like work, stop thinking that way. You're mistaken if you think it shouldn't be this hard. Do the work, trust yourself, and just watch who and what shows up for you. If creating a new approach to finding love sounds a little scary and confronting—good! You're moving in the right direction. This is about exploration and the hunt. You're going to have a hell of a lot of fun, and the invitation is to be playful throughout.

"Why is it so hard to find a good man?" Renya asked during a discovery session with me. "I've had it with men! They're all losers, and all they want is sex." Renya was dejected and frustrated. She's a fiery woman with a heart of gold broken way too many times to count. She is a highly successful event planner, and it's her job to (*a*) plan, (*b*) find people to make the event happen, and (*c*) make her customers happy. She was looking in all the wrong places for him. She also was **looking from** the wrong place. This will make more sense later.

Grab a Flashlight!

"Well, where the hell are they?" Renya snarkily spoke into the phone, replying to me. So I asked a different question, "Well, Renya, where have you been looking?" Perplexed by my question, she asked what I meant. This began the exploration into where Renya was looking for and looking from. It's subtle but an essential distinction in your quest for love.

There are two places we look to find a partner. We look for the person in our world through our life experiences and look for this person from a place within us shaped by our experiences. From within, we're shaped by (*a*) our history of relationships, (*b*) what we know and don't know, and (*c*) what we believe is possible or not. You can implore several strategies for both approaches. In this chapter, I'll share a few. We'll practice a little common sense as we bring in the power of the Universe, the woo-woo, and the magic. All hands on deck, okay? I invite your open mind and heart here. Ready? Are you willing?

Duh, Go Where They Are

One of my best friends, Nate, was single for years. With a few relationships under his belt, he was perplexed why he couldn't find his ideal partner. It was as if he set himself up to fail repeatedly. By settling or creating unwinnable games in the search for his partner, he was consistently left not creating the relationship he wanted. He was finally ready to approach finding his next relationship differently.

He hired a coaching colleague, and they explored what he wanted. He spent some time getting super clear, painfully clear—about (*a*) the characteristics his future partner would possess, (*b*) what the experience was like being with her, (*c*) what she would look like, (*d*) what she did, (*e*) what her emotional temperament was, and (*f*) how they would partner together during the day-to-day comings and goings of life—all of it. They created a future vision, and Nate began living daily in that vision.

Nate is an incredible athlete, insanely fit, and able to push his body to physical limits most of us can only dream about. He's a super handsome, brilliant man who owns his own business. A total package kind of guy. Although he was sought after by quite a few women at any given moment, he was ready to play a bigger game and get the forever partner he wanted.

As committed to fitness as Nate was, he was equally attracted to a particular female physique—the CrossFit body: a big booty, thick legs, chiseled features, calloused hands, and incredible physical strength. Most of all, Nate was attracted to the mental rigor required to be a high-performing, CrossFit athlete. Grit, determination, and dedication are some of the most attractive features for Nate. However, time and time again, Nate went on dates with women who didn't have those characteristics—not even close. They lacked the physical strength and grit Nate found so attractive.

So where were these women? Nate longed and longed to be around these women. I asked one day, "If you're so attracted to this type of woman, why don't you spend more time where they are?" They're at the CrossFit gyms; it was a simple but powerful realization. Six months later, he met her. They now compete together and support each other in the competitions they take on. From all appearances, they seem incredibly happy to have found each other.

I share Nate's story for one simple reason. If you're attracted to a specific type of woman, man, or person, spend more time where they will be. Take classes and go to events or locations where they're found. Begin to explore how to find them by looking where they will be. Put yourself out there in new ways. Remember, if you want a different result, it will require different effective actions. This isn't a mind-blowing discovery, but it is so simple it's often overlooked. Go where they are. Keep going and keep exploring.

Are You to Blame?

You may be the one at fault here. Inevitably, you're partly to blame, at the very least. It will be hard to overcome if you keep thinking about your story of how hard it is to find the right person. Congratulations! If you have a narrative about how all the good ones are taken, they'll all be taken. Congratulations! If you're like Renya from earlier in this chapter, you'll only attract losers and people who want to screw you. All these beliefs and stories perpetuate your sucky relationships or even a lack thereof. It's time to profoundly alter the story you've told yourself.

Your thoughts materialize and create your experience. This was not-so-common sense for Nate, who simply went where **they** were, but it could be. It should be common sense since this is powerful knowledge. Your mind is an incredibly effective tool at shaping your reality. What you believe, you'll achieve. Your thoughts will become your reality. You cannot alter the story of your past or how your present experiences have unfolded. But you have all the power of the universe to change the future. Your adventure starts with how you think, speak, and behave within your current relationship paradigm. Your happiness is at stake.

Mahatma Gandhi famously said, "Happiness is when what you think, what you say, and what you do are in harmony." If today is the day you begin to practice aligning your thoughts, speech, and actions to do what it takes to find your love and happiness in a relationship, then keep reading.

For the next week, I have a practice for you to notice your thoughts, words, and actions. Notice this specifically: do these thoughts, words, and actions come from love or fear? They likely have been coming from fear up to this point. Yes, there have been episodes of them coming from love, but you probably wouldn't be reading this book if fear had not dominated you. There is a fear-based belief under all those thoughts, words, and actions that you won't find your person. You'll die alone as a hermit or with ten cats known as that weirdo on the block in your neighborhood. So for the next week, examine whether fear or love drives your thoughts, words, and actions. The goal here is to ensure they're all driven by love.

Look at some examples of speech that would be driven by love versus fear:

◆ "This book is bullshit, and another thing that won't help me" (fear)
◆ "My person is out there, and I'm learning to bring them to me" (love)
◆ "I am just going to mess it all up anyway" (fear)
◆ "I am willing to explore and try something different" (love)

Spend the next week noticing if you're behaving from fear or love. Just notice, don't judge. Don't make yourself wrong for behaving from a fearful place and celebrate yourself when your behavior comes from a place of love. Simply notice and name it. Once you've developed some efficiency here by noticing and naming your fear and love behaviors, the next action is to practice choosing. Choose fear or choose love. By now, you should be very familiar with the payoff when you choose fear. You get to be **right,** and life is predictable. It is known. Choosing love will likely be outside your comfort zone, so by definition, it will be uncomfortable. This is where the possibility of love lives. Choose in the face of discomfort. Are you willing?

Who Are They?

Are you ready to place your order? Do you understand who your partner needs to be for you to be completely satisfied? Every aspect of their being will be explored. The questions below will support you in your exploration. Feel free to add any additional comments. Answer these questions as a writing exercise. Get as specific and detailed as possible:

◆ What do they look like, i.e., physical characteristics and features?
◆ What do they smell, feel, and taste like? (Yes, taste—assuming you'll have your mouth on them at some point.)
◆ What do they do for a living? How do they make money?
◆ What do they do in their spare time?
◆ How do they interact with others?
◆ How do they treat others?
◆ How do they treat you?
◆ How do they dress?
◆ What makes them laugh?
◆ What makes them sad?

Now spend some time exploring the experience of what it is like to be with them:

◆ What is it like to come home to them?
◆ How do they make you feel when they embrace you?
◆ What are you sharing together?
◆ How do they make your life easier?
◆ How do they make your life more challenging?
◆ Do they make you want to be your best self?
◆ How do they bring joy, love, and abundance to your life?
◆ How will they make you sad?
◆ How will they break your heart?
◆ How will they make you cry?

Spend as much time as you want and need. Approach this as your order to the Universe (your wish list) and what you're manifesting to come into your life. I've no idea how or why this works, but it does. Getting to this level of clarity will support you when—not if—your person shows up. If you're telling yourself you already did this (with a vision board, workshop, future vision, or whatever), do it again. This practice is not about arriving at a destination; it's not just a one-and-done effort. This is a practice of being on the journey to continuously explore, create, and attain your partner. It is also a practice of making yourself experience, in real time, what it would be like to finally be with this person.

Magic Everywhere

The law of attraction, manifestation, visualizations, future visions, and the like will be your guides. Countless books have been written about this simple, universal truth: if you want something, then believe you already have it. Neither a wish nor a desire, but a belief you already have it. Believe it with all your heart and with every fiber of your being. This works for everything: love, money, abundance, fame, and possessions. These aren't my rules; they're the rules of the Universe.

It's critically important to understand how your thoughts, words, and actions will impact what comes to you. For example, how often have you stated that you want a better relationship or find your forever partner? The critical word here is **want**, and wanting is how most of us unknowingly sabotage ourselves. When your thoughts, words, and actions are created from **a want**, you'll create the experience of wanting. Did you catch that?

You're getting exactly what you put out into the Universe. You have created the experience of wanting a better relationship. Now, the magic starts to happen if you can act according to the Universal Truth by acting as if this experience is currently realized.

Acting **as if** you're currently living your vision seems simple enough, but it will take diligent practice. Think that you already possess this relationship. Speak as if it's here and occurring in your daily life. Act **as if** your person is already in your life. You may notice some resistance right now—good. This is your logical, comfort-zone brain resisting the opportunity of taking a new and different action. You're on to a new awareness and a new way of being. Lean into this opportunity. I had a client go so far as to purchase his wedding band. He wore it every day, acting as if he was already in the relationship he wanted. He was diligent about not wearing it on dates and in places where he had an opportunity to meet someone; nevertheless, he still practiced **as if**. He's had a few incredible women show up in his life, but he still hasn't quite met the one—yet.

They Are You

Looking within yourself to find your person is as critical as looking where they may be. This is your work and an opportunity to create the relationship experience you want from within you. What I'm referring to is clarity. Like Nate, you must get painstakingly, crystal clear on who this person is for you. This clarity will allow the forces of the Universe to bring this experience and person to you.

Here's the kicker: to have the person and experience you want, you must be that for yourself first. Yep—if you want love, then be loving. If you want joy, then be joyful. If you want a super attractive, fit, successful partner, then be that for yourself. You'll attract what you are and who you're being. Be the person you want to be with (for you and them).

Don't Give Up Even When You Fuck Up

You may fail as you fall back into old patterns during your journey. So you may get close to (*a*) finding the person that you want, (*b*) having the experience that you want, and (c) showing up as the person you want to be while you are your person. Close, but no cigar.

When this happens, just acknowledge that you've created a relationship that isn't meeting the conditions to leave you satisfied. Then remove yourself from that relationship and get back to work. Intuition is vital in supporting you.

It is going to be exciting to think you've found your person. The joy, fun, passion, infatuation, lust, sex, and new conversations will be a welcome experience compared to how past relationships have occurred as you trudged the road to find love. Then you'll experience shock when you realize the person you're currently in a relationship with may not be your **person**. The red flags creep in, and the little voice says to go, but for some reason, you may be unwilling to end it and start over again.

This is predictable, but you'll need to demand what you want. Another relationship that doesn't get you what you want won't serve you. You've been there and done that. Get uncomfortable; say the **bold thing**. If the relationship can be reinvented—great! If not, then you need to move on. Are you willing to make that deal with yourself?

Authenticity

Finally, let's talk about authenticity. Being the real you for real. Notice when you may be performing—acting as if you're someone you're not by hiding the insecure, unevolved, scared parts and holding back your powerful, unique self from love. Acting stronger than you may feel, exaggerating how cool and sexy you are, or leaving your convictions by the wayside, so you don't rock the boat with your new beloved sets you up for future failure.

From day one, be you. There is only one you in the entire universe. You have unique gifts and experiences to share and create. Don't forget that. There is nothing wrong with you and nothing that needs to be changed for you to give and receive love. There may be some work to do to elaborate on that experience, but you are you. Honor that.

Inauthenticity will lead to more inauthenticity. Before you know it, you'll have lost yourself in this process. Then you'll have to start reading this book over again from the beginning. Once you've found the one, you'll begin this new relationship by creating the juiciest, most loving, and most fearfully vulnerable experience of a partnership you can imagine. Turn the page. That's where we're going next.

CHAPTER SIXTEEN

CREATING PARTNERSHIP

> "Never above you, never below you, always beside you."
> - Walter Winchell

What do I mean when I use the word **partnership**? I believe partnership is (*a*) the experience of moving through life with someone, (*b*) to have and to hold, (*c*) to pick up where the other stops, and (*d*) to lift up when the other falls. A partner fills our gaps. We all have gaps, as Rocky Balboa so brilliantly shared with Paulie while punching a side of beef in the blockbuster movie *Rocky*. "Together, we fill gaps," he said. That's the essence of a partnership. The partner fills in where the other stops and vice versa. Partnership is the reason we seek a person to love and be loved by as we live our daily lives. When we have a partner, we have someone, and, in turn, we're someone to another. It gives us and our lives meaning and a place for our heart and soul to land as we hurl through space on this giant rock called Earth. We mean something. We matter. Having togetherness, shared goals, purpose, meaning, a ride or die, or a bae is an opportunity to understand who you are and who you are not at your core. This understanding is essential when it comes to creating a partnership. The Gottmans, the researched-based relationship gurus of The Gottman Institute, emphasize that partnership is an agreement of co-creation. From this agreement, goals are subsequently born, then meaningfully shared. This co-creative agreement is the **most meaningful** aspect of a partnership. The achievement of these goals is a bonus. I agree wholeheartedly, and creating the shared meaning, and the shared intention with your chosen person takes understanding, vulnerability, and courage.

To begin, we need to lay a firm foundation. Knowing the level of partnership we desire and having a clear understanding of what partnership is – is where many of us kind of fuck up the whole experience of our romantic relationships. We go into a relationship with vague ideas about what we truly want. Is this the right person to give us what we're not even clear about? Ha! See how you're already screwed or beginning to screw it up?

So where do we falter, and how can the experience be created differently? My intention in this chapter is to explore what it takes to lay your firm foundation. Then notice how you may set yourself up for disappointment. Then create a structure not to do that. We'll look at the story of my client, Ellen. I'll also share a bit about my experience screwing up my relationships and how I got clear on creating a partnership I was courageous enough to build with my wife.

Partnering Self

First, become the best damn version of yourself for you—no shit, no kidding—for real. Create a partnership with yourself that's rock solid so you can be sincere when you realize there's still work to do. This is about being responsible. It's being the best for yourself first, then for your potential partner. Have you heard the saying, "How can you love someone else if you don't love yourself first?"

How can you expect the best of another person—a person you choose to partner with—if you're not showing up as the best version of yourself? Debbie Ford, the brilliant author of *The Dark Side of the Light Chasers: Reclaiming Your Power, Creativity, Brilliance, and Dreams,* shared the premise we must know and embrace all of ourselves (the dark, the light, the good, and the bad) to love and accept ourselves. This is what I mean about being responsible and demanding excellence from yourself. You must get to know **all of you**. Know your limitations and where you excel. Know what triggers your anger and sadness. Also, know your ability to trigger others' anger and sadness. Demand excellence from yourself before placing expectations on another person. Do you! Do your self-development work, be a partner to yourself first, then create a partnership with another. So get curious about yourself and how you usually create relationships.

- Where do you let yourself off the hook (physically, emotionally, mentally, spiritually)?
- Where is your work? Where are your gaps?
- Is there some old harm or trauma a therapist needs to address with you?
- Have you let your body go and need to take control of your health?
- Do you have a spiritual life and practice?

Get curious and courageous while you demand excellence from yourself.

Expectations

Your happiness is in direct proportion to your expectations. There is so much truth in this statement. If you expect more than your partner can deliver, you'll consistently feel let down, and your needs will routinely go unmet. While in the relationship or initial courting stages, come to understand who your partner is and is not. That goes for you too. Fully understand who you are and who you aren't while creating a partnership. I can't tell you how often I've heard clients say, "If only my partner would do/be this/that way, then everything would be fine."

Remember (and I say this with love)...you chose them. You did! You now get to be responsible for how you choose and continue to choose your partners. What made you choose a partner who may be incapable of meeting your needs? Unfortunately, this is the point where many lovers sabotage any true sense of creating a partnership from the moment they first lock eyes. Is it possible your loneliness blinded you to the red flags or the feeling in your gut silently screaming, "Hey! This **isn't** your person!"?

You may have strategically planned their transformation in the back of your mind. You were figuring out how to change them to satisfy your conditions for your ideal partner. You intended to fix and mold them into a masterpiece—you...the sculptor; they...the clay.

There is inherent sabotage with this approach because this person probably won't be able to change to meet your needs. Remember those needs? You forgot their importance. You lowered your expectations. It happened when he or she went beyond a few dates and committed to you. This is a consequence of choosing someone below your conditions of satisfaction. Honor your expectations and be honest about who you've chosen or will choose.

Creating expectations in a partnership takes acceptance and willingness. Accept your partner for who they are. Also, accept that your partner may not fit your needs. This acceptance **must happen**. Go ahead and do the same for yourself. Be willing to (*a*) be with, (*b*) love, and (*c*) accept all of yourself.

Communication is vital and will be discussed in this chapter. Put this conversation on the loudspeaker and create how you want your relationship to go with your partner. Sit with your partner and outline your expectations about what it means to be together. It may take personal growth and/or additional support from outside the relationship, but **get real** with what each of you expects from the other. Have a candid conversation, then do the writing exercises at the end of this chapter and have fun. Agree about how your partnership will progress and how each of your expectations will or won't be met by the other.

Intentionality

Great partnerships don't just happen. They're made, created, invented, and—yes—they take work. We often get stuck in the magical thinking that it shouldn't be hard; or take effort if it's meant to be. I believe creating a solid relationship with courage and heart requires shared intentions from both people. In the corporate world, this is called having a mission, a vision, and a purpose. The same applies here. Have an intention and goals you agree upon for creating your partnership. It will be crucial when you navigate the roller coaster of love and your life. Without it, there's no compass or direction. You, the Universe, and your future partner will have no idea how to find you. There's no road map for success if you lack shared intentions. There's no purpose for the relationship to exist.

Here's a story about how my lack of intention manifested in others. Many years ago, once my heart healed a bit after a breakup, I felt lonely since the relationship ended unexpectedly. Being relatively clueless and unaware at the time regarding how unhappy my partner was, our breakup stunned me. One day, I was picking her up for dinner, and she asked me, "Hey, can you just park so we can talk?" Yes, it was **that talk**.

Weeks of devastation followed, then I began feeling increasingly lonely. My heart hurt terribly; however, we were at least honest about acknowledging we were on a path to Nowheresville. She took action to solve our intentionless, unfulfilling partnership. She was the honest, brave one. She spoke the scary words, and, just like that, I was single again.

A few weeks passed, and while the grief of my lost, imagined future made the breakup more real, I noticed how much I missed being touched— not in an entirely sexual way, although that was part of it. I simply missed feeling someone feel me. It was almost primal and animalistic. I missed being hugged, holding hands, being kissed, the light caress on the back of my arm, the hand on the back of my neck, and the cheek-to-cheek touch. I missed the romantic, human connection and—yes—the sex.

I believed distracting myself with a sexual encounter would support me in getting over my fresh, new ex. As a disclaimer, I don't recommend using sex as a tool for healing or getting over someone, but I was a completely different, untransformed man back then compared to the man I am today. I was doing my best with what I had at the time. My intention wasn't to get into another relationship but to have fun, distract myself, and meet my physical needs.

With the advent of online dating apps, finding someone to go on a date with whom you may end up having sex with is pretty easy. After a few hours, I had plans to meet a woman for coffee. It was crystal clear neither of us intended to create a partnership. We just wanted to feel less alone for a night.

Alice was beautiful and easy to talk with. We quickly connected over conversations about the Chicago music scene, riding bicycles while dodging the distracted drivers flying down the busy streets, and our shared love of dessert. We went on a few dates and even had a conversation acknowledging that we both knew it was going nowhere. There was no long-term intention for either of us, yet we both found each other. We had an on-and-off sexual fling for a couple of months until we disappeared from each other's lives. We fulfilled the purpose of our meeting. The point is you'll attract what you seek—period. Getting clear about the partnership you want and being willing to create it is one of the most important, magical acts of this process. Be the person you want your partner to be, then watch them show up.

When I met my wife, Shona, my intentions were 100 percent different. I wanted a relationship. I wanted to meet my forever partner, and I started speaking, thinking, and behaving like it. Amazing women began entering my life. I went on some dates. I created new online profiles on dating apps. My intention was known. "I'm Looking for Her" was prominent in my profile, and when I met these women, guess what happened? I began attracting more women who also intended to create a strong and loving relationship— women ready for commitment and the creation of a partnership.

I still got the occasional late-night, "you-up?" text, the equivalent of a booty call. But I didn't engage. It was out of alignment with the integrity of my new intention. I was looking for her, and she showed up. If you're uncertain about what you want, then stop. Get crystal clear. Make it clear that it's known to you, the Universe, and your future partner about what you want and don't want. Create your intention and watch who shows up.

Creating Your Definition of Partnership

Part of creating what you want is to find a partner who understands your true definition of partnership. What is it? How will you know when you create it? How will you know when you're out of partnership with your chosen person? These are all critical questions. You must understand the answers to create a meaningful experience with another human being.

In the exercises at the end of this chapter, spend time creating your definition of partnership. Explore what the experience of sharing your life with another person is truly about for you. Why would you? Why are the two of you together? How will you interact when one of you shows up as less than their best? Keep asking questions. I invite you to ask questions of yourself and your current or future partner. If there's a gap in your experience, then bridge it. Find common ground to agree upon and a barometer to gauge your partnership's success or failure. Decide when there's something to work on or when there's cause for celebration. You'll probably fall in and out of partnership over time. So notice it and normalize it. Choose with whom you'll both be moving forward together in a partnership.

Love Languages

Understanding how you and your partner give and receive love will be critical in developing a lasting partnership. It's one of my favorite questions to ask new clients. I'm shocked many can't answer it and have never asked their partner. Many think it's one love language when it's actually another. There are a gazillion resources to discover your love language. Discover it, then find your current or future partner. The concept of love languages was developed by bestselling author Gary Chapman, who asserts that each of us prefers to receive love in different ways. The five love languages include

◆ Quality time,
◆ Physical touch,
◆ Giving acts,
◆ Acts of service, and
◆ Words of affirmation.

We tend to give love the way we like to receive it. However, this may be out of alignment with how your partner (or future partner) receives love. You may think you're meeting the love needs of your partner when you're failing miserably.

Ever hear, "The way to a man's heart is through his stomach!" or "Diamonds are a girl's best friend!"? These sweeping beliefs guide us to assume we know what needs to be done to make the other person feel adequately loved. It's not true for everyone. So never make assumptions.

I'm reminded of Jeff and his wife, Adele. Their relationship regressed to one of bickering roommates when I started coaching Jeff. He was like a wounded animal, blaming his wife for everything. He constantly lashed out, complained, and even considered throwing in the towel. There was much finger-pointing at her for not being responsible for his part in the relationship breaking down. Once we honored, heard, and processed his complaints, we moved away from them and gained some elevation. It came down to the fact he felt uncared for and unloved. Adele wasn't meeting his needs for love. So I invited them to understand better how they each loved to be loved. They started exploring. Jeff was starving for words of affirmation, while Adele showed her love in acts of service. Adele was dying for giving actions, and Jeff was all about physical touch. They weren't loving each other because they didn't know how. Once they understood they didn't know how to love each other, we created practices for each. Quickly the bitterness and bickering cleared up. I couldn't believe how fast their partnership turned around. It hit home for me to recognize the importance of truly understanding how each person wants to be loved. Choose to love your partner as they want to be loved. Start now.

Communication

"We just don't talk anymore" was one of the first comments Ellen shared during our initial discovery session. She found me through social media and wanted to explore coaching. She said she was impressed with the relationship I have with my wife. Looking at the pictures we shared and capturing the good parts of our relationship, she knew there was a possibility of gaining a better relationship than she currently had with her husband, Gabriel. Her marriage was near the end of the road. She and Gabriel were considering divorce after twelve years of partnership.

Ellen is a fantastic woman with a hippieish, bohemian vibe; she's caring, driven, and powerful as all hell. She's all heart, and there's a lot of joy in her eyes. She leads a large department for a healthcare company and commands a large team while handling what needs to be done. At work, she has a voice and unshakable confidence, but for some reason, that voice and spirit were left at the office when she arrived home to the husband she began to resent.

She spent the last couple years of marriage with no voice and feeling a constant tug on her heart for a more meaningful, fulfilling experience of love. Her unmet needs and inability to communicate with her husband resulted in falling into an abyss of resignation and "fuck its!"

"This is just the way it is!" she exclaimed, "No matter how hard I try, there's no changing him."

Hold up! Stop! That's it right there! We aren't in the game of changing our partners. We know from experience and how we've set our expectations this is a form of sabotage. It's a setup for resentment, anger, fear, and retaliation. A true partnership cannot be created by trying to fix sabotage. When I asked her if she had brought her concerns to her husband, she quickly shot back, "No! He should know what I need!"—a complete communication breakdown. One of the primary purposes of effective communication in relationships is to get our needs met. Period.

The word **should** is a killer of so many relationships. It's the flag-bearer of resentment and unmet needs, and we must become responsible for removing it from our lexicon. We say:

◆ "My partner should do this."
◆ "She should have known that."
◆ "They should have remembered."

The **shoulding** all over our partners happens far too often. Stop it—seriously! It's irresponsible because it lets you off the hook from asking for what you need.

Ellen and I quickly identified she wasn't asking for what she needed. Once we understood why she wasn't asking, it became clear what she needed to do next. Outside the **shoulding**, there was an underlying context/thought/belief that Ellen was holding on in her partnership with Gabriel. There was a tiny thought in her mind that she didn't matter. Was it true? Of course not, but the thought needed to be revealed to name it so she could choose differently when relating to herself and Gabriel. So why was she holding her worth and value in such low esteem? What was the point of asking for what she needed? Can you see the setup for Ellen not getting her needs met? Ellen needed to first demand her value and worth herself before approaching her needs with Gabriel. Her current cycle of partnership looked like this: (*a*) my needs aren't being met, (*b*) I'm not asking my partner to meet them, (*c*) I don't believe I'm worthy of having my needs met, (*d*) my needs continue to go unmet, (*e*) I become needy, and (*f*) I should on my partner.

Be responsible for communicating what you need to your partner. Be reasonable about what you ask for, knowing your chosen partner's limitations and boundaries. Remember you chose him or her. Choose wisely. I'm not saying that all of it has to be you; both people need to take action to improve communication for either one to get their needs met. Is it that easy? Yes, it can be; but for some, it may seem like an alien landscape as they drift in space. The unknown makes them feel unsure, scared, and confused. So consider taking small steps at first.

When my wife, Shona, and I were navigating the first few months of our relationship, we quickly recognized the importance of giving our needs a voice. We've had pretty good success. Sometimes it takes a few days, weeks—hell—**months** to flesh out what each of us needs. One or both of us may know there's a need but finding a voice for it can be like detonating a bomb with a pair of tweezers or a sledgehammer. We recognized this gap and created an amusing way to let each other know there's a conversation to be had—a need to be addressed.

This was also an opportunity to reinvent how we approached our communications and our partnership in general. So we bought an elephant. We did! No, it's not an actual elephant. It's a super-tacky, fake, jewel-encrusted ceramic elephant that fits in the palm of my hand. It's our beacon that something is going on. One of us has a need to voice and is having a hard time communicating. So it's a direct request: "Hey, we need to talk!" If it's placed by one of us on our dining room table, then we both know that there's a communication breakdown. We need to take time to connect and just be with what the other person has to say. It's neutral territory too. Anything can be brought up without judgment or criticism. We make the time no matter what. Our elephant is a little support structure we created to improve and build upon our partnership and communication. Would a similar support structure like the elephant Shona and I created help you and your current or future partner?

The critical takeaway is to acknowledge that your relationship will slowly or rapidly degrade if you don't create a system to talk to each other about anything at any time. A primary purpose of communication in relationships is to provide a platform to share your needs with your partner. This is the foundation of a successful relationship.

You may wonder how Ellen and Gabriel ended up. After a few months of coaching, Ellen found herself and her voice. She began communicating her needs to Gabriel. It was a huge breakthrough and an event worth celebrating; however, time and time again, Gabriel was unable to meet her needs. The needs she stated weren't unreasonable. So Ellen had to choose to either stay in a relationship that proved it didn't meet her needs or end the relationship. As challenging and heartbreaking as it was, she ended it. The last time we connected, she was happier than she had been in years. A brand-new future is available to her as she now (*a*) communicates, (*b*) takes responsibility for her happiness, and (*c*) gets her needs met. She's dating again, knowing that she matters, and she shares her needs with a powerful voice.

Breakdown—It Happens

So what do I mean when I say breakdown? In the simplest terms, a breakdown happens when something stops working. My car breaks down; my computer breaks down. Either an event occurs, or a line in the sand must be drawn. Enough is enough. Something broke. A breakdown is an awareness that something in a relationship needs attention and needs it quickly because something isn't working. Breakdowns are a gift; they're alarm bells that something needs to happen or needs attention—**stat!** This can have any level of significance. A breakdown is an opportunity for you and your partner to (*a*) notice the dynamic playing out in your relationship, (*b*) name the breakdown, (*c*) own what made it happen, (*d*) choose who both of you'll be about it, and (*e*) recommit to something new and inspiring around your vision of partnership.

I can guarantee there will be a time you and your partner will have a breakdown. Life happens. We're human and we make mistakes. We falter on our commitments and fuck up, and it's okay. There needn't be any additional significance put on the breakdown. Be with it and feel it. Just as our bodies produce a fever to fight off an illness, a breakdown is an opportunity to fight off more damaging actions, thoughts, or behaviors. It doesn't have to define you, your partner, or your relationship. Welcome and acknowledge breakdowns because you'll discover they're fresh soil for growth if you choose to view them as an opportunity.

Declaring a breakdown takes awareness, courage, and elevation. Embrace it and bring your words from love and understanding. There's nothing wrong if you look at it as a way to grow and get closer to each other. Then choose to reinvent your relationship dynamic around what contributed to the breakdown in the first place. You'll see some practices below to complete as a writing exercise. They have been developed to add clarity to create your own exciting, joyful partnership.

Partnership Practices

1. What is your definition of partnership?
2. How do (or will) you practice partnership with your person?
3. What are the expectations of you and your partner?
4. What is your (and your partner's) love language?
5. What are your current needs that are going unaddressed?

6. What support structure (elephant) will you employ to facilitate communication?
7. Are there any current breakdowns to declare with yourself or your partner?
8. What actions will you practice to overcome your breakdown?

Finally, realign the relationship to the highest vision of your partnership. You get a say, your partner gets a say, and you work to make it better. There is limitless access to love and joy in partnership with the person you've chosen. It's possible, and I believe in you.

CHAPTER SEVENTEEN

THOUGHTS ON SPIRITUALITY

> "Your trials didn't come to punish you but to awaken you."
> - Paramahansa Yogananda

I felt compelled to include a chapter on spirituality in this book. I exist. You exist.

I believe there is something else out there greater than all of us: the Universe, Spirit, God, intuition, three-eyed spaghetti monster, a doorknob—whatever you want to call it. You may begin to cringe at the topic while other readers feel curious, welcome, and at home. I intend to share my relationship with spirituality to demonstrate the power that can be yours in your quest for love and happiness. I don't have an agenda, nor am I looking for converts to the cult of Conlin Coaching and *Why My Relationships Suck*. I'm inviting you to simply explore, be open, and see if there's any value here for you.

First, I want to share an important distinction. When I use the term spirituality, I'm not referring to organized religion. I find the two are each distinct, but they can be mutually exclusive. Both can play different roles in your life and relationship experiences. Many people have a challenging relationship with religion. That's the experience of many people I meet and one I had myself back in the day. Today I'm at peace with religion and its followers. This won't be an academic or philosophical dissertation. Exploring the religion that (*a*) you grew up with, (*b*) was given to you by your parents, or (*c*) traumatized or harmed you in some way isn't the purpose of this chapter.

I worked with Jason for a few months, helping him remove the roadblocks in his dating life. He held fast to the familiar belief there must not be anyone for him. Every woman he met wasn't **the one**. He was painfully lonely and becoming increasingly resigned in the process. Jason, by definition, was a great guy. He had all the essentials: a good job, money in the bank, and a lovely home. He was physically fit and had a kind face. He's a good dude, but his heart was incredibly guarded and closed off. When I pried my way in, he'd play dumb. His default reply to uncomfortable questions was, "I don't know, man." Whenever I heard it, I knew he was protecting himself.

I asked about his relationship with Spirit. "I don't know, man. I don't have one," he replied as defensiveness crackled in his voice.

"Have you ever?" I asked.

"I guess so, but I don't want to go to church, and I don't believe in God," he replied.

"Got it. I'm not asking those questions," I said. "I'm just asking if you feel connected to something outside yourself—something other than yourself."

"I never thought of it like that," he replied as his shield came down.

As the conversation with Jason continued, we uncovered some pain and trauma he associated with God and religion. I reminded him we were talking about Spirit. He could explore it without defending himself or feeling angry. He could examine the pain and trauma another time, likely with a therapist if he was willing. I asked him to consider creating a relationship with Spirit, a force outside himself and see if it could support him.

"Do you see some value in leaning into Spirit?" I asked.

"Man, I'm up for anything, but this feels like nonsense," Jason shared.

"Can you feel the nonsense and create value anyway?" I coached. "What's the value you see here?"

"Not sure, but I'm open to anything," Jason offered.

"Great! So, in action, what does this look like?" I asked.

Jason was willing. He was willing to see how a spiritual practice could support him in his life. I shared what worked for me in the past and what was currently working.

He began creating his practice. During our time together, Jason became less emotionally heavy, for lack of better terms. He developed a new resolve and a sense of hope, which brought power into his life and what he was working on for his relationship project. He created the experience that he wanted. Spirituality became something to lean into that supported him. It's as simple as that, and that's the invitation. Create something—anything—you can lean into, even if it feels nonsensical. Keep trusting in and watch what happens.

To be clear, I don't speak ill of religion, discredit religion as a construct, or belittle any specific religion. I don't care. I'm one man with one experience and one opinion. In my understanding, religion is **a way** to connect with spirituality and have a spiritual practice, but it doesn't have to be **the way**. With most of clients, there exists a relationship with Spirit. Whether it's a strained relationship, a thriving one, or one of seeking, there's something to explore. So it makes sense to explore it, right?

My aim is for you to see your relationship with Spirit for what it is. Understand how it may or may not support you in finding the love you want. Hang in there. Be open. Be curious. And just be with it. Remember... we are in a relationship with everyone and everything. How you are or how you show up in all your relationships is worth investigating, especially if, time and time again, you find you're not getting what you want.

God is an Asshole

For much of my adult life, I didn't understand the difference between religion and spirituality. I didn't care to understand. I was raised in a semi-religious home. We went to church on Sundays, I went to Catechism (of the Catholic Church) on Wednesdays, and I even went through a few of the sacraments from the Seven Sacraments of the Catholic Church. My religious practice was a chore I **had to do,** so I never saw any value. That feeling and what came next resulted in abandoning religion and spirituality altogether. To me, God turned into a gigantic, fucking asshole.

God took my dad. He murdered my dad. One day Dad went to work, but he never came home, and then he died. I blamed God for his death. I shared the death of my father earlier in this book and the associated grief my mother felt but didn't share how I ultimately blamed God. I needed a target for all my sadness, blame, and anger. I had to make sense of it. My childish brain couldn't process what happened. I kept thinking he'd come home any day or Dad was lost somewhere. I dreamed I'd find him and escort him home to repair our broken family—a dream I occasionally still have.

My seething anger was brutal. It consumed me in various ways throughout much of my life. As a seven-year-old boy, it expressed itself as confusion and social and emotional withdrawal. As I got older, the rage, self-destructive tendencies, and substance abuse took the place of confusion and withdrawal. I got in fights and began physically harming myself by cutting and punching anything until I bled. Ultimately, my expression of anger ended in addiction, bewilderment, and codependency.

So what does this have to do with spirituality? I found spirituality through my devastating circumstances. My anger, the destruction of my body, and my addiction became like religion. It brought me to understand a version of Spirit— what some people call God—and how I'm connected to something divine.

I can believe in something greater than myself, which makes me feel more connected; and secure in that belief. The Universe, intuition, the law of attraction, Spirit, God, faith, coincidence, miracles, déjà vu—whatever it is—it is. It helps me (*a*) move through fear, (*b*) grow and discover deeper levels of trust, and (*c*) love and be loved in deeper, more profound ways. This is my hope for you: to see you gain a connection to something during the process of finding or improving your experience of love and relationships. As you know, the process of finding love can get lonely. You can become consumed with the despair of yet another failed relationship, the frustration from another terrible date, and the worry about another piece of evidence that makes you feel like, yes, there's something wrong with you. One of the biggest benefits of connecting to a spiritual practice is that you'll eventually feel less alone. You'll grow a connection to what you choose is natural for you, and you will find ease in being you. Choose and bring your intention to your relationship to Spirit—fake it until you make it if you must.

When I Almost Died

I came to understand my concept of spirituality after losing everything in life. I felt beaten down and had nowhere to go. I was burned up, busted out, and zigzagging through life. I had nothing left to lose, so I figured I'd see if there was any value in developing a spiritual practice. During recovery, I was encouraged to develop a relationship with something greater than me that was outside of myself. I remember thinking, "If this is the solution to help me, then I'm fucked!"

Intuition told me resistance and unwillingness to create a spiritual practice and life could kill me. I surrendered to the possibility there was something outside myself to believe in and connect with. It felt ridiculous like I was a fool to even consider it. My self-sufficiency and reliance on willpower were all I knew, but that same reliance on willpower almost killed me. It was indeed a dark time in my early thirties.

I was killing myself by abusing drugs and alcohol. There was a time when I wanted to feel anything except what I felt. It was absolute insanity. I was stealing, lying, and behaving in ways I would never dream of behaving now. I was sick, totally sick, living a life my heart knew was wrong. However my head kept feeding the addiction, constantly talking me into bad decisions and actions. In hindsight, I realize I wasn't willing to start a healing journey yet. The pain and trauma kept festering inside. I was using drugs and alcohol to medicate the pain and provide a distraction.

I was out of control, consumed by fear, and unable to ask for help. Just a few days away from an unplanned, lethal overdose, I'm certain a heartbreaking death would've been my fate. Writing this now, it terrifies me that I was that man. A man who went to those lengths of dread and despair and **almost killed himself** over not being willing and humble enough to ask for help. I thought I'd figure it out eventually, but that day never came. I'm so grateful to those who saw my pain and held an intervention. It's been over a decade since I quit abusing drugs and alcohol, but that man is still within. The man who craves connection, a sense of belonging, trust, faith that I'll be taken care of, and the reassurance that everything will work out.

When it all came crashing down, I was relieved. Forced to get help, I finally was beaten down enough to accept it. With that relief also came utter devastation. In one week, I was fired from my job, and my wife asked for a divorce. I had to sell my home and car and was admitted into a treatment program. I spent the next four months getting well, trying to figure out how the hell it happened. I was better than that; I knew better and wasn't raised to fail.

Just Another Relationship

My relationship with a spiritual practice could be mirrored by any relationship I've experienced. Sometimes I feel supported, basking in the goodness of Divine connection. At other times, I feel alone, afraid, and disconnected—cursing the Universe, Spirit, God, or whatever else you want to call it. The same events that brought me to my knees also brought a spiritual realization. Simply put, I needed help—a lot of it—and needed it everywhere: medically from doctors and nurses who cared lovingly for me, emotionally from the army of therapists and counselors who started my trauma healing, and spiritually from something greater than me.

So why would you want to develop or deepen a spiritual practice when it comes to creating the relationship that you want? First, that's a great question: Ask yourself, **"How could a spiritual practice support me in creating the relationship I want?"** Take a moment and answer it for yourself.

What did you come up with? The answer to this question is almost always as unique as the person who asks it. There's no right answer. Embracing a spiritual practice in my relationship process allowed taking on more risk. I felt supported and connected to do big, scary acts as I looked for the woman and experience of my dreams. When I was rejected for the one-hundredth time, catfished by another online profile, or ghosted after a few dates with a woman I genuinely liked, I had a relationship that mattered to fall back on—my connection to Spirit and the associated practice.

I held on to the faith (*a*) of someone being out there for me, (*b*) in the knowledge that there truly was nothing wrong with me, and (*c*) I was both loved and lovable. When I felt lonely and sad, there was a place to feel those feelings. I took it to my spiritual practice. I processed what I felt and grounded myself in what I wanted and was creating.

Remember, spirituality can be whatever you want it to be—whatever works **for you.** The beautiful part is you get to create spirituality. The goal of spiritual practice is to feel and be connected. Simple, right? Your brain and past experience of spirituality or religion will probably want to complicate matters. It will try to make it bigger than it needs to be or explain it away as an absurdity and nonsense.

My first experience creating a spiritual practice came during treatment. I needed something to connect to that wasn't me and not someone else. I had a life full of people who were shocked, disappointed, and concerned for me. It was too much to consistently go to them for support. My best thoughts and actions landed me in a frickin' rehab unit, so I knew I couldn't get what I needed from me. I leaned into nature, allowing myself to be in it and explore its wonders more than ever before.

An old oak tree outside my window became my first spiritual practice. Each morning, I sat on the floor and looked out the window. I traced the tree branches, starting from the trunk to the thickest branches. Then I traced the smaller ones and even smaller ones until I was tracing the skinniest twigs. I repeated this process until I outlined the entire tree.

I don't know why this became my ritual and practice, but every morning, I began to feel better. Hope started growing within. I started feeling less afraid and alone. No matter what, I could always go back and trace the tree. I started falling in love with nature and began noticing it everywhere. More present to its beauty and complexity, I started feeling a part of nature and less alone.

It May Look Different

In my opinion, a belief in Spirit (discovering something bigger outside yourself) gives you access to greater power—the power to believe, have faith, and trust that you'll get what you want. I've found many times in life, and in the lives of clients, it doesn't always look like what we think it should. It also doesn't look like what we want it to look like. If you're open to it, then it will come to you in some form. The result you want may not look like the result you expected.

When I was dating my wife, I didn't expect her to be **the one.** She was right in front of me in my home, sitting on the couch. I stood in the kitchen watching her. It was mid-October, and she was drawing a face on a pumpkin we were going to carve. On paper, she was **the one**—yes, **the one!**—although I wasn't quite ready to receive her. I became confused, scared and began to withdraw. I was convinced I'd never find the right woman, although she was sitting on my damn couch.

I brought my confusion and fear to my spiritual practice, meditated on it, asking for guidance to remove the blocks. I discovered I feared commitment, disappointment, rejection, and another damn catastrophe of a heartbreak. It became clear those feelings were in the way. The right woman—**the one**—was in front of me, and I couldn't see her. Leaning into Spirit again gave me the clarity and the courage to believe what I wanted in a relationship and a partner was possible.

On our fourth date, we were enjoying dinner together. The restaurant was an amazing French bistro in the hipster part of town. Shona looked gorgeous. She has the most beautiful eyes, and the shape of her face triggers a primal attraction in me. She's my definition of beauty, and every part of me was into her, yet I still resisted fully committing to her. As I watched her enjoy her dinner, a soft whisper said, "You're going to marry her."

I turned around, shocked because no one was there. I heard the voice as clear as day and could have sworn the waiter came by playing a magic trick. I came to believe this was Spirit guiding my search for love. Neither my humanity, the past, nor my fear would've ever seen the woman sitting there as **the one.** It would've been impossible because I didn't believe in her or in myself.

Leaning into my spiritual practice guided me and provided the confidence to move forward. That evening, I took myself off all dating apps and committed the rest of my life to her. She didn't know I was her husband yet, but I did.

A Ritual

One of the biggest benefits of creating a spiritual practice is the ritual. Along the lines of grounding yourself when you're scared, alone, or feel resigned, the ritual is one of the most comforting, supportive practices you can create for yourself. After all, ritual is in the word spiritual. Create a practice for you...by you. It doesn't have to look any particular way but create it.

I've found meditation is a powerful practice for me. When I first began meditating, I envisioned what I thought it should look like: forty-five minutes twisted into the lotus position on a mat in complete stillness, achieving enlightenment—yeah...bullshit! What meditation looks like in **real life** is sitting on a chair in my living room for ten to twenty minutes, wrestling to keep my mind quiet while I receive intuitive guidance about the next steps to take in my life. Some days I wrap up meditation feeling fully restored and energized. On other days, I feel like it was a waste of time. Either way, I'm in practice. I'm practicing what supports me. With practice, it gets better. I get better benefits, and it reinforces new behaviors. If you've ever played sports or a musical instrument, you know you get better with practice and repetition. The same applies to a spiritual practice. Practice it. Practice discovering what it means for you, and don't stop.

Remember, this time is for you. It is meant to be the practice that brings you closer to your beliefs, desires, and internal landscape. Go deep, be open, and receive what comes to you. Your practice is meant to guide your actions and support; then you take on new challenges while moving through old ones. Here are some ways to get started:

◆ Discover a ritual that feels right for you.
◆ Set aside time to practice it (daily, weekly, in the moment—whatever).
◆ Create a journal to record the outcome of your practice.
◆ Write down what you notice, feel, and believe as a result.
◆ Explore how you can grow and deepen your practice.
◆ Finally, write down the reasons to grow and deepen your practice.

If you're feeling completely stuck, consider starting small. Take baby steps. When I first started, I'd take three deep breaths. I'd notice what came up in my head and heart, then I'd take one last deep breath. That was it. Then I got on with my day. Sometimes I did it sitting or lying in bed before getting up in the morning. I might do it over the kitchen sink multiple times throughout the day—whatever, whenever, and wherever. It took less than a minute, and I did it every day.

I can't explain or guarantee what you'll gain from opening up to a spiritual practice. Creating your ritual and being open will cause a shift, even if it's simply feeling more relaxed from the deep breathing. It will produce a benefit by deepening how you see and feel about yourself.

Magic happens, and a sense of connectedness and belonging ensues. Trust and faith begin pulling you through the hardest times, and you become free. As you go on your journey, consider creating a relationship to Spirit as an opportunity—one that may support you and your heart.

Be honest. Be open. Be willing. Watch what begins to happen. You'll be astonished at what comes to you before you're even halfway through: **big love.**

Conclusion

The seed for *Why My Relationships Suck* was planted out of despair after a lifetime of heartbreak and failed relationships. This book blossomed and began to grow when I created the most loving, healing, compassionate, and courageous relationship I've ever experienced: the relationship with myself. It was a relationship I purposely and courageously created. You'll create this type of relationship with yourself and those you choose to love.

I hope to help you begin your self-love journey by reading this book. You have now been equipped with tools to take responsibility for your relationships. You now have a choice to take bold, courageous actions in service of the love you've yearned for (likely) most of your life. You've been given a specific set of tools to clear away the debris of your past relationships that sucked. You've learned to see your past heartbreaks as gifts leading to your healing and the closing of your gaps as you find love. You've discovered the patterns that no longer serve you and likely swallowed huge chunks of truth about yourself. You've gained clarity on what and who you want while understanding the person you yearn for and the experience you want is almost definitely outside your comfort zone. You've seen where courage is needed and compassion and forgiveness are required. Hopefully, you see what you want through receiving help from others, the Universe, Spirit, and a god of your understanding. You've come to believe love is possible.

The old cliché "Love is possible only when you choose to love yourself first" is true. Your journey of discovery about what it means to practice loving yourself has begun. You possess the ability to love yourself through the discomfort of future terrible dates and inevitable heartbreaks to ultimately find the one person your soul has guided you toward your entire lifetime. Choosing to love yourself has allowed you to find the love of your life.

The goal of this book is to help you start your journey. It's just the beginning. I hope you see the value in your healing journey and begin unraveling the past that has kept you in a pattern which no longer serves you. I also hope you see value in working with a professional coach to lovingly push you toward your future, outside your comfort zone. You're unlikely to fully embrace different actions without the support of another person.

Finally, I hope you see the remarkable miracle of a human being you are. There is no other you on the planet. You're a gift worthy of immense, unconditional love—not only from within but also as expressed through others. You'll have challenging times ahead and glorious ones as well. This is life. Be with it all. Practice trusting the process, and please don't stop. You're guaranteed not to get what you want if you stop. By continuing to move forward, all possibilities remain available. Best wishes on your journey, and please consider this book and me as a resource at any point you need.

Thank you,

ABOUT THE AUTHOR

I have lived this journey; it's one marked by a long history of failed relationships. Like my failed marriage, I had an overall failure to understand—even about who I was. What I thought I wanted in life and love often left me at a crossroads of loneliness and despair. Time and time again, I would notice the patterns in my life led me to another unfulfilling relationship, complete with the inevitable broken heart. "Why?" I thought, "How can this happen differently?" I learned I was creating love all wrong. I was looking outside myself for a fulfilling, loving relationship. It wasn't until I began the journey of self-discovery and created a relationship with myself that it was possible to make it happen differently. This journey allowed me to not only meet but also be ready for the one.

I support others in their love-seeking journeys by freely sharing my story and the stories of those I've helped. If you want another relationship book written by a Ph.D., a therapist, or a marriage counselor, then this is not your book. Drop it now, move along, and thanks so much for looking. However, if you want to share a journey with someone who's been in the trenches of creating love, devastated, broken to a million pieces, and fortunate enough to recover and create the most fulfilling relationship and marriage ever, then let's go! I'm your guy! Together we will embark on a journey of love, self-discovery, wonder, and creation.

I live in Chicago with my miracle son, Forest, and my amazing, brilliant, beautiful, and patient wife, Shona. I spend most of my days coaching and supporting others because it is me living my life's purpose. I'm challenged every day to show up powerfully and lovingly in all my relationships. That, too, is my life's purpose and a lesson I continue to practice and learn.

This challenge dares me to be kinder and grow to become more loving with myself and those I get to love. I actively work the 12 Steps in two programs to support my addictive, codependent tendencies. I'm better when I'm working the Steps. I enjoy playing music and spending as much time as possible being in nature. Nature is my safe place. It has been since I was a child. I'm grounded in nature.

My work and approach to how I love and create relationships has been shared globally. I've been featured on *ABC World News Tonight*, *The Tamron Hall Show*, *CBS This Morning*, *Good Morning America*, NBC, many international media affiliates, and almost every social media platform that exists. Just search for my name and for "The Date Night Dad."

My whole heart goes out to you. May you find love worthy of the miracle that you are.

Big love,
Bob Conlin

REFERENCES

Chapman, G. (2015). The 5 Love Languages: The Secret to Love That Lasts. Northfield

Publishing; Reprint edition (January 1, 2010).

Fane, B. (2015). Grief Symptoms: How Grief Affects the Brain. Retrieved from https://barbarafane.com/grief-symptoms-how-grief-affects-the-brain/

Fisher, H., Aron, A., & Brown, L. (2006). Romantic Love: A Mammalian Brain System for Mate Choice. Retrieved from https://www.ncbi.nlm.nih.gov/pmc/articles/PMC1764845/